History of Flagellation Among Different Nations

Strange Customs and Cruelties of the Romans, Greeks, Egyptians, etc.

by Jaques Boileau
(1635-1716)

with an introduction by Dahlia V. Nightly

This work contains material that was originally published in 1888.

This publication is within the Public Domain.

This edition is reprinted for entertainment purposes
and in accordance with all applicable Federal and International Laws.

Introduction Copyright 2018 by Dahlia V. Nightly

CREDITS & ACKNOWLEDGEMENTS

Front Cover -
König David tut Buße (King David Does Repentance) by Albrecht Dürer
[Public Domain],
via Wikimedia Commons

Back Cover -
Weiditz Trachtenbuch des Christoph Weiditz
Germanisches Nationalmuseum Nürnberg, Hs. 22474. Bl.
69-70 Jungfrau in Barcelona, von hinten gesehen / Kastilianischer Büßer (Geißler)
http://dlib.gnm.de/item/Hs22474
(Manipuliert, um das buch in doppelseiten anzuzeigen)
[Image enhanced by Black Books]
via Wikimedia Commons

Black Books Logo -
Candle Collection by VectorPocket, via FreePik.com *(Cropped)*
Vanitas [Painting] by Bartholomäus Bruyn the Elder, Public Domain *(Cropped)*
Marbled Pedestal with Old Books by Kues1, via FreePik.com (Cropped)

Research / Sources -
Wikimedia Commons
www.Commons.Wikimedia.org

Many thanks to all the incredible photographers, artists,
researchers, and archivists who share their great work.

PLEASE NOTE :
As with all reprinted books of this age that are intended to perfectly reproduce the
original edition, considerable pains and effort had to be undertaken to correct fading and
sometimes outright damage to existing proofs of this title. At times, this task can be quite
monumental, requiring an almost total rebuilding of some pages from digital proofs of
multiple copies. Despite this, imperfections still sometimes exist in the final proof and
may detract slightly from the visual appearance of the text.

DISCLAIMER :
Due to the age of this book, some methods or practices may have been deemed unsafe or
unacceptable in the interim years. In utilizing the information herein, you do so at your
own risk. We republish antiquarian books without judgment or revisionism, solely for
their historical and cultural importance, and for educational purposes.

Strange Arts for Dark Hearts

Black Books
PUBLICATIONS

Introduction

We at *Black Books* are pleased to bring you another rare, fascinating old find – this time a book on flagellatory practices across the world.

This special edition of ***History of Flagellation Among Different Nations : Strange Customs and Cruelties of the Romans, Greeks, Egyptians, Etc.***, was written by Jaques Boileau, and first published in 1888, making it 130 years old.

This antiquarian text features a fascinating insight into the practice of flagellation as a punishment and a penance, among various nations and cultures, including Christians, Egyptians, the Romans, Greeks.

This old book is an absolute must-have for all those interested in world history in general, and in corporal punishment, and the darker side of religion in particular.

Strangely yours...

~ *Dahlia V. Nightly*

State of Jefferson, July 2018

ELOQVENTIA
VERAX

PREFACE.

A period will, sooner or later, arrive, at which the disciplining and flagellating practices even now in use, and which have been so for so many centuries, will have been laid aside, and succeeded by others equally whimsical. And while the men of those days will overlook the defects of their own extravagant customs, or perhaps even admire the rationality of them, they will refuse to believe that the practices of which accounts are given in this work, ever were in use among mankind, and even matter of great moment among them. The design, therefore, is effectually to remove all doubts in that respect, by handing down to them the flower and choice parts of the facts and arguments on the subject.

This book will likewise be extremely useful to the present age; and it will in the first place be so, the subject being considered in a moral light. The numerous cases that are produced in this book, of disciplines which offenders of all classes, kings as well as others, have zealously inflicted upon themselves, will supply a striking proof of that deep sense of justice which exists in the breasts of all men; and the reader will from such facts conclude, no doubt with pleasure, that even the offenders of the high rank we have just mentioned, notwithstanding the state by which they were surrounded, and the majestic countenance which they put on, sometimes in proportion as they more clearly know that they are wrong, are inwardly convinced that they owe compensation for their acts of injustice.

If considered in a philosophical light, this work will be useful to the present age, in the same manner as we have said it would be to posterity.   The present generation, will find in it proofs both of the reality of the singular practices which once prevailed in various countries, and are still in full force in many others, and of the important light in which they have been considered by mankind.   They will meet with accounts of bishops, cardinals, popes, and princes, who have warmly commended such practices; and will not be displeased to be moreover acquainted with the debates of the learned on the same subject, and with the honest, though opposite, endeavours of a Cerebrosus and a Damian, a Gretzer and a Gerson.

We may add that the principal part of the facts and anecdotes are taken from the very rare work of the Abbe Boileau.

History of Flagellation.

CHAP. I.—*The use of Flagellations known among the
ancient heathens.*

IT is not to be doubted, that flagellations had been
invented, and were become, in early times, a common
method of punishment in the Pagan world. Even before the
foundation of Rome, we meet with instances which prove
that it was the usual punishment inflicted on slaves. Justin,
in his epitome of Trogus Pompeius, relates that the Scythians
more easily overcame their rebellious slaves with scourges and
whips, than with their swords. "The Scythians being returned
(says Justin) from their third expedition in Asia, after having
been absent eight years from their wives and children, found
they now had a war to wage at home against their own slaves.
For, their wives, tired with such long fruitless expectation
of their husbands, and concluding that they were no longer
detained by war, but had been destroyed, married the slaves who
had been left to take care of the cattle; which latter attempted
to use their masters, who returned victorious, like strangers, and
hinder them, by force of arms, from entering the country. The
war having been supported for a while, with success pretty
nearly equal on both sides, the Scythians were advised to change
their manner of carrying it on, remembering that it was not
with enemies, but with their own slaves, that they had to fight;
that they were to conquer by dint, not of arms, but of their
right as masters; that instead of weapons, they ought to bring
lashes into the field, and, setting iron aside, to supply themselves
with rods, scourges, and such like instruments of slavish fear.

Having approved this counsel the Scythians armed themselves as they were advised to do; and had no sooner come up with their enemies, than they exhibited on a sudden their new weapons, and thereby struck such a terror into their minds, that those who could not be conquerred by arms, were subdued by the dread of the stripes, and betook themselves to flight, not like a vanquished enemy, but like fugitive slaves."

Among the ancient Persians, the punishment of whipping was also in use : it was even frequently inflicted on the grandees of the kingdom by order of the king, as we find in *Stobæus*, who moreover relates in his forty-second discourse, "that when one of them had been flagellated by order of the king, it was an established custom, that he should give him thanks as for an excellent favour he had received, and a token that the king remembered him." This custom of the Persians was however in subsequent times altered ; they began to set some more value on the skin of men; and we find in Plutarch's *Apothegms of Kings*, "that Artaxerxes, son of Xerxes, surnamed the *Longhanded*, was the first who ordered that the grandees of his kingdom should no longer be exposed to the former method of punishment; but that, when they should have been guilty of some offence, instead of their backs, only their clothes should be whipped, after they had been stripped of them."

We also find, that it was a custom in ancient times, for generals and conquerors, to flog the captives they had taken in war; and that they moreover took delight in inflicting that punishment with their own hands on the most considerable of those captives. We meet, among others, with a very remarkable proof of this practice, in the tragedy of Sophocles, called *Ajax Scourgebearer:* in a scene of this tragedy Ajax is introduced as having the following conversation with Minerva.

MINERVA.—"What kind of severity do you prepare for that miserable man ? "

Ajax.—I propose to lash his back with a scourge till he dies."

Minerva.—"Nay do not whip the poor wretch so cruelly."

Ajax.—"Give me leave, Minerva, to gratify, on this occasion, my own fancy; he shall have it, I do assure you, and I prepare no other punishment for him."

Flagellation Customs.—The Romans.

The punishment of flagellation was also much in vogue among the Romans; and it was the common chastisement which judges inflicted upon offenders, especially upon those of a servile condition.   Surrounded by an apparatus of whips, scourges, and leather straps, they terrified offenders, and brought them to a sense of their duty.

Judges, among the Romans, as has been just now mentioned, used a great variety of instruments for inflicting the punishment of whipping.   Some consisted of a flat strap of leather, and were called *Ferulæ;* and to be lashed with these *Ferulæ,* was considered as the mildest degree of punishment. Others were made of a number of cords of twisted parchment, and were called *Scuticæ.*   These *Scuticæ* were considered as being a degree higher in point of severity than the *Ferulæ,* but were much inferior in that respect, to that kind of scourge which was called *Flagellum,* and sometimes the *Terrible Flagellum,* which was made of thongs of ox-leather, the same as carmen used for their horses.   We find in the third satire of the first book of Horace, a clear and pretty singular account of the gradation in point of severity that obtained between the above-mentioned instruments of whipping.   In this satire, Horace lays down the rules which he thinks a judge ought to follow in the discharge of his office; and he addressed himself, somewhat ironically, to certain persons who, adopting the principles of the Stoics, affected much severity in their opinions, and pretended that all crimes whatever being equal, ought to be punished in the same manner.

"Make such a rule of conduct to yourself (says Horace) that you may always proportion the chastisement you inflict to the magnitude of the offence; and when the offender only deserves to be chastised with the whip of twisted parchment, do not expose him to the lash of the horrid leather scourge, for that you should only inflict the punishment of the flat strap on him who deserves a more severe lashing, is what I am by no means afraid of."

The choice between these different kinds of instruments, was, as we may conclude from the above passage, left to the judge, who ordered that to be used which he was pleased to name; and the number of blows was likewise left to his discretion; which sometimes were as many as the executioner could give. "He (says Horace in one of his Odes) who has been lashed by order of the Triumvirs, till the executioner was spent."

Besides this extensive power of whipping exercised by judges among the Romans, over persons of a servile condition over aliens, and those who were the subjects of the republic, masters were possessed of an unbounded one with regard to their slaves, over whose life and death they had moreover an absolute power. Hence a great number of instruments of flagellation, besides those above mentioned, were successively brought into use for punishing slaves. Among those were particular kinds of cords manufactured in Spain, as we learn from a passage in an Ode of Horace, the same that has just been quoted, and was addressed to one Menas, a freed-man, who had found means to acquire a great fortune, and was grown very insolent. "Thou (says Horace) whose sides are still discoloured (or burnt) with the stripes of the Spanish cords."

A number of other instances of this practice of whipping slaves, as well as other different names of instruments used for that purpose, may be found in the ancient Latin writers, such as Plautus, Terence, Horace, Martial, &c.   So prevalent had the above practice become, that slaves were frequently denominated from that particular kind of flagellation which they were most commonly made to undergo.   Some were called *Restiones*, because they were used to be lashed with cords; others were called *Buccædæ*, because they were usually lashed with thongs of ox-leather; and it is in consequence of this custom, that a man is made to say in one of Plautus' plays, "they shall be *Buccædæ* (that is to say, scourged with leather thongs) whether they will or no, before I content to be *Restio*," or so much as beaten with cords.   And Tertullian, meaning in one of his writings to express slaves in general, uses words which simply signify "those who are used to be beaten, or to be discoloured with blows."

Nay, so generally were whipping and lashing considered among the Romans, as being the lot of slaves, that a whip, or a scourge, was become among them the emblem of their condition.   Of this we have an instance in the singular custom mentioned by *Camerarius*, which prevailed among them, of placing in the triumphal car, behind the Triumpher, a man with a whip in his hand; the meaning of which was to show, that it was no impossible thing for a man to fall from the highest pitch of glory into the most abject condition, even into that of a slave.

Suetonius also relates a fact which affords another remarkable instance of this notion of the Romans, of looking upon a whip as a characteristic mark of dominion on the one hand, and of slavery on the other.   "Cicero (says Seutonius, in the life of Augustus) having accompanied Cæsar to the Capitol, related to a few friends whom he met there, a dream which he had had the night before.   It seemed to him, he said, that a graceful boy came down from heaven, suspended by a golden chain; that he stopped before the gate of the Capitol, and that Jupiter gave him a whip *(flagellum.)* Having afterwards seen Augustus, whom (as he was still personally unknown to several of his near relations) Cæsar had sent for and brought along with him to be present at the ceremony, he assured, his friends that he was the very person whose figure he had seen during his sleep." Juvenal likewise, in one of his satires, has spoken of Agustus conformably to the above notion of the Romans. "The same (says he) who, after conquering the Romans, has subjected them to his whip."   But, besides all those instruments of flagellation used for punishing slaves, which have been mentioned above, and as if the terrible *flagellum* had not been of itself sufficiently so, new contrivances were used to make the latter a still more cruel weapon; and the thongs with which that kind of scourge was made, were frequently armed with nails, or small hard bones.   They also would sometimes fasten to those thongs small leaden weights: hence scourges were sometimes called *Astragala*, as Hesychius relates, from the name of those kind of weights which the ancients used to wear hanging about their shoes.   Under the tortures which those different instruments inflicted, it was no wonder that slaves should die: indeed this was a frequent case; and the cruelty, especially of mistresses towards their female slaves, grew at last to such a pitch, that a petition was made in the Council of Elvira to restrain it; and it was ordained, that if any mistress should cause her slave to be whipped with so much cruelty as that she should die, the mistress should be suspended from communion for a certain number of years.   The following are the terms of the above ordinance, in the fifth canon. "If a mistress, in a fit of anger and madness, shall lash her female slave, or cause her to be lashed, in such a manner that she expires before the third day, by reason of the torture she has undergone; inasmuch as it is doubtful whether it has designedly happened, or by chance; if it has designedly happened, the mistress shall be excommunicated for seven years; if by chance, she shall be excommunicated for five years only; though, if she fall into sickness, she may receive the communion."

Roman Gallants Punished by Flagellation.

The absolute dominion possessed by masters over the persons of their slaves, led them to use a singular severity in the government of them. So frequently were flagellations the lot of the latter, that appellations and words of reproach drawn from that kind of punishment, were, as hath been above observed, commonly used to denominate them; and expressions of this kind occur in the politest writers: thus, we find in the plays of Terence, an author particularly celebrated for his politeness and strict observance of decorum, slaves frequently called by the words, *Verberones, Flagriones,* or others to the same effect.

As for Plautus, who had been the servant of a baker, and who was much acquainted with everything that related to slaves, and their flagellations in particular, he has filled his scenes with nicknames of slaves, drawn from this latter circumstance; and they are almost continually called in his plays, *flagritribœ* (a verbis, *flagrum and terre) plagipatidœ, ulmitribœ, &c.,* besides the appellations of *Buccœdœ* and *Restiones,* above mentioned.

Sometimes the flagellations of slaves, or the fear they entertained of incurring them, served Plautus as incidents for the conduct of his plots; thus, in his *Epidicus,* a slave who is the principal character in the play, concludes upon a certain occasion, that his master has discovered his whole scheme, because he has spied him, in the morning, purchasing a new scourge at the shop in which they were sold. The same flagellations in general, have moreover been an inexhaustible fund of pleasantry for Plautus. In one place, for instance, a slave, intending to laugh at a fellow-slave, asks him how much he weighs, when he is suspended naked, by his hands, to the beam, with an hundred-weight *(centupondium)* tied to his feet; which was a precaution taken, as commentators inform us, in order to prevent the slave who was flagellated from kicking the man *(Virgator)* whose office it was to perform the operation. And in another place, Plautus, alluding to the thongs of ox-leather with which whips were commonly made, introduces a slave engaged in deep reflection on the surprising circumstance of " dead bullocks, that make incursions upon living men."

Vivos homines mortui incursant boves !

But it was not always upon their slaves only that masters, among the Romans, inflicted the punishment of flagellation: they sometimes found means to serve in the same manner the young men of free condition, who insinuated themselves into their houses, with a design to court their wives. As the most favourable disguise on such occasions, was to be dressed in slave's clothes, because a man thus habited was enabled to get into the house, and go up and down without being noticed, rakes engaged in amorous pursuits, usually chose to make use of it ; but when the husband either happened to discover them, or had had previous information of the appointment given by his faithful spouse, he feigned to mistake the man for a runaway slave, or some strange slave who had got into his house to commit theft, and treated him accordingly. Indeed the opportunity was a most favourable one for revenge ; and if to this consideration we add that of the severe temper of the Romans, and the jealous disposition that has always prevailed in that country, we shall easily conclude that such an opportunity, when obtained, was seldom suffered to escape, and that many a Roman spark, caught in the above disguise, and engaged in the laudable pursuit of seducing his neighbour's wife, has, with a *centuponium* to his feet, been sadly rewarded for his ingenuity. A misfortune of that kind actually befel Sallust the Historian. He was caught in a similar intercourse with Faustina, wife to Milo, and daughter of the Dictator Sylla. The husband caused him to be soundly lashed *(loris bene cæsum);* nor did he release him till he had made him pay a considerable sum of money. The fact is related by Aulus Gellius, who had extracted it from Varro. To it was very probably owing the violent part which Sallust afterwards took against Milo, while the latter was under prosecution for slaying the Tribune Clodius, and the tumult he raised on that occasion, which prevented Cicero from delivering the speech he had prepared.

An allusion is made to the above practices in one of Horace's satires. He supposes in it, that his slave, availing himself of the opportunity of the *Saturnalia,* to speak his mind freely to him, gives him a lecture on the bad courses in which he thinks him engaged, and uses, among others, the following arguments.

" When you have stripped off the marks of your dignity, your equestrian ring, and your whole Roman dress, and from a man invested with the office of judge, shew yourself at once under the appearance of the slave Dama ; disgraced as you are, and hiding your perfumed head under your cloak, you are not the man whom you feign to be: you are at least introduced full of terror, and your whole frame shakes through the struggles of two opposite passions. In fact, what advantage is it to you, whether you are cut to pieces with rods, or slaughtered with iron weapons ? "

The above uncontrolled power of inflicting punishments on their slaves, enjoyed by masters in Rome, was at last abused by them to the greatest degree. The smallest faults committed in their families by slaves, such as breaking glasses, seasoning dishes too much, or the like, exposed them to grievous punishments; and it even was no unusual thing for masters (as we may judge from the description of *Trimalcion's* entertainment in the satire of Petronius) to order such of their slaves as had been guilty of faults of the above kind, to be stripped, and whipped in the presence of their guests, when they happened to entertain any at their houses.

Women in particular seemed to have abused this power of flagellation in a strange manner; which caused express provisions to be made, at different times, in order to restrain them; of which the canon above quoted is an instance. It was often sufficient, to induce the Roman ladies to cause their slaves to be whipped, that they were dissatisfied with the present state of their own charms; or, as Juvenal expresses it, that their nose displeased them: and when they happened to fancy themselves neglected by their husbands, then indeed their slaves fared badly. This latter observation of Juvenal, Dryden, in his translation of that author's satires, has expressed by the following lines:

> "For if over night the husband has been slack,
>   Or counterfeited sleep, or turn'd his back,
>   Next day, be sure, the servants go to wrack."

Here follows the literal translation of the passage of Juvenal, in which he describes in a very lively manner, the havoc which an incensed woman usually made on the above occasion. "If her husband has, the night before, turned his back on her, woe to her waiting woman; the dressing maids lay down their tunics; the errand slave is charged with having returned too late; the straps break on the back of some; others redden under the lash of the leather scourge, and others, of the twisted parchment."

The wantonness of power was carried still farther by the Roman ladies, if we may credit the same Juvenal. It was a customary thing with several among them, when they proposed to have their hair dressed both with nicety and expedition, to have the dressing maid who was charged with that care, stripped naked to the waist, ready for flagellation, in case she became guilty of any fault or mistake, in performing her task. The following is the passage in Juvenal on that subject. " For, if she has determined to be dressed more nicely than usual, and is in haste, being expected in the public gardens, the unfortunate Psechas then dresses her head, with her own hair in the utmost disorder, and her shoulders and breasts bare. Why is that ringlet too high ? The leather thongs instantly punish the crime of a hair, and an ill-shaped curl."

. These abuses which masters, in Rome, made of the power they possessed over their slaves, were at last carried to such a pitch, either by making them wantonly suffer death, or torturing them in numberless different ways, that, in the beginning of the reign of the Emperors, it was found necessary to restrain their licence.

Under the reign of Claudius (for it is not clear whether any provision to that effect was made under Augustus) it was ordained, that masters who forsook their slaves when sick, should lose all right over them, in case they recovered; and that those who deliberately put them to death, should be banished from Rome.

Under the Emperor Adrian, the cruelties exercised by Umbricia, a Roman lady, over her female slaves, caused new laws to be made on that subject, as well as the former ones to be put in force, and Umbricia was, by a rescript of the Emperor, banished for five years.

New laws to the same ends were likewise made under the following Emperors, among which civilians make particular mention of a constitution of Antoninus Pius *(Divus Pius);* and in subsequeut times, the church also employed its authority to prevent the like excesses, as we may see from the canon above recited *(Si quæ domina, &c.)* which was framed in the Council held at Elvira, a small town in Spain, that has been since destroyed. But the disorder was of such a nature as was not to be cured so long as the custom itself of slavery was allowed to subsist; and it has been remedied at last, only by the thorough abolition of an usage which was a continual insult on humanity: an advantage which (to be, once at least, very serious in the course of this learned and useful work) we are indebted for, to the establishment of Christianity, whatever other evils certain writers may reproach it with having occasioned.

ANECDOTES OF ANCIENT SCHOOLMASTERS.

The punishment of flagellation was thought among the ancient heathens, as we have just seen, to possess great efficacy .to mend the morals of persons convicted of offences, and insure the honesty and diligence of slaves. Nor were schoolmasters behindhand either with judges or masters, in regard to whipping those persons who were subjected to their authority.

Of this we have an undoubted proof in one of the epistles of Horace; and it moreover appears that he had had, when at school, the bad luck of being himself under the tuition of one who had strong inclinatiou to inflict that kind of chastisement. " I remember (says he) that the flogging Orbilius, who when I was a boy, used to dictate to us the verses of Livius Andronicus."

.......Memini quæ plagosum mibi parvo
Orbilium dictare.—Lib. II. Ep. i. v. 70.

Quintilian has also mentioned this practice of schoolmasters of whipping their disciples; and the severity which they used, as well as other considerations, induced him to disapprove of it entirely. The following are his expressions on that subject. "With respect to whipping schoolboys, though it be an established practice, and Chrysippus is not averse to it. First, it is a base and slavish treatment; and certainly if it were not for the youth of those who are made to suffer, it might be deemed an injury that might call for redress. Besides, if a disciple is of such a mean disposition that he is not mended by censures, he will, like a bad slave, grow equally insensible to blows. Lastly, if masters acted as they ought, there would be no occasion for chastisement; but the negligence of teachers is now so great, that, instead of causing their disciples to do what they ought, they content themselves with punishing them for not having done it. Besides, though you may compel the obedience of a boy, by using the rod, what will you do with a young man, to whom motives of a quite different nature must be proposed? Not to add, that several dangerous accidents which are not fit to be named, may be occasioned either by the fear or the pain attending such punishments. Indeed, if great care is not taken in choosing teachers of proper dispositions, I am ashamed to say to what degree they will sometimes abuse their power of lashing: but I shall dwell no longer on that subject, concerning which the public know already too much."

After these dismal accounts of disciples flogged by their teachers, and of the cruel severity used by the latter, the reader will not certainly be displeased to read instances of teachers who were flogged by their disciples.

A very remarkable instance of this kind occurs in the case of that schoolmaster of the town of Falerii, who is mentioned in the fifth book of the Decad of Livy. The town of Falerii being besieged by the Romans, under the command of the Dictator Camillus, a schoolmaster in that town, thinking he would be splendidly rewarded for his service, one day, led, by treachery, and under pretence of making them take a short walk out of the gates of the town, the children of the most considerable families, who had been entrusted to his care, to the Roman camp, and delivered them up to the dictator. But the latter, incensed at his perfidy, ordered him to be stripped naked, with his hands tied behind his back, and having supplied the children with rods, gave the schoolmaster up to them, to drive him back in that condition to their town.*

Another instance of the like kind is also to be met in more modern times. The tutor's name was Sadragefillus, and his disciple was Dagobert, son of Clotaire, king of France, who reigned about the year of Jesus Christ, 526. The translation is related in the following manner by Robert Gaguin, in his History of France. "Dagobert (says he) having received from his father a tutor who was to instruct him in the worldly sciences, and whom the king had made the duke of Aquitain, the young man, who did not want parts for one of his years, soon perceived that Sadragefillus (such was the pedagogue's name) was much elated with pride on account of his newly acquired dignity, so that he began to fail in the respect he owed to

---

* Denudari deinde Ludi-magistrum jussit, eumque pueris tradidit reducendum Falerios, manibus post tergum illigatis; virgas quoque eis dedits, quibus proditorem agerent in urbem verberantes.

The inhabitants of Falerii were so struck with the just conduct of the Dictator (Livy adds) that a total change of their dispositions towards the Romans was the consequence; and the senate having been assembled thereupon by the magistrates, they came to the resolution of opening their gates, and surrendering to the Romans; which was soon after effected.

him, and grew remiss in the discharge of his duty.   The prince
having once invited him to dine with him, and Sadragefillus
having not only placed himself at the table opposite the prince,
but also offered to take the cup from him as if he had been
his companion, the prince ordered him to be soundly whipped
with rods, and caused his beard, which he wore very long,
to be cut off."   The above fact is also related by Tilly, scrivener
of the parliament of Paris, in his chronicles of the kings of
France.

In fine, to the passages above produced concerning the
flagellations of children, from which we find that very great men
have much differed in their opinions in regard to them, we
may add, that king Solomon, that oracle of wisdom, has, without
reserve, declared in favour of that mode of correction. "He
that spareth the rod, hateth his son; but he that loves him
chastises him betimes."   The Greek philosopher, Chrysippus has
afterwards manifested the same opinion.   And Petrarch, who
may be called here a modern author, has also adopted the
opinion of king Solomon; and notwithstanding Quintilian's
arguments on the subject, has sided with the ancient moralist
and sage: "correct your son (says Petrarch) in his tender
years, nor spare the rod: a branch when young may easily
be bent at your pleasure."

CHAP. II.—*Flagellations of a religious and voluntary kind were practised among the ancient heathens.*

WE have hitherto only treated of involuntary flagellations, and such as were in all cases inflicted by force on those who suffered them. But besides flagellations of this kind, there were others of a voluntary sort among the heathens, to which those who underwent them, freely and willingly submitted, and which may indeed create our surprise in a much greater degree than the former.

Thus, at Lacedæmon, there was a celebrated festival, which was kept annually, and was named the Day of Flagellations, on account of the ceremony that was performed in it, of whipping before the altar of Diana, a number of boys, who freely submitted to that painful treatment; and this festival has been mentioned by a great number of authors.

Plutarch, for instance, in his book of the customs of the Lacedæmonians, relates, that he had been an eye-witness of the celebration of the solemnity we speak of. "Boys (says he) are whipped for a whole day, often to death, before the altar of Diana the Orthian; and they suffer it with cheerfulness, and even with joy: nay, they strive with each other for victory; and he who bears up the longest time, and has been able to endure the greatest number of stripes, carries the day. This solemnity is called the Contest (or race) of Flagellations; and is celebrated every year."

Cicero, in his Tusculana, has also mentioned this custom of the Lacedæmons. "Boys (says he) at Sparta, are lashed before the altar in so severe a manner, that the blood issues from their bodies. While I was there, I several times heard it said that boys had been whipped to death; none of whom ever uttered the least complaint, though lacerated by repeated lashes." Nay more; Mozonius, in Stobæus, relates that the Spartan boys were rather pleased with these flagellating solemnities. "The sons of the Lacedæmonians make it very evident (says Mozonius) that stripes do not appear to them either shameful or hard to be borne, since they allow themselves to be whipped in public, and take a pride in it."

The scholiast or commentator of Thucydides relates the same things of the Lacedæmonian young men; and says that those among them who could bear the greatest number of lashes, acquired much glory by it. "And indeed (says he) the flagellations are performed at particular times during a certain number of days; and those who receive the greatest number of stripes, are accounted the most manly." The parents of the young men who were thus publicly whipped, were commonly present during the performance of the ceremony; and so far were they from discouraging their sons from going through it, that, as Lucian relates, they deemed it a shameful piece of cowardice in them, if they seemed to yield to the violence of the lashes, and in consequence of this notion they exhorted them to go stoutly through the whole trial. "Indeed (continues Lucian) a number of them frequently died in the conflict, thinking it was unworthy of them, so long as they continued to live, to yield to blows and bodily pain, in sight of their friends and relations." "And to those who die upon those occasions, statues as you will see, are erected at Sparta, in the public places."

Seneca, in his treatise upon Providence, has also mentioned those singular flagellations which took place at Lacedæmon, as well as the conduct of the Lacedæmonian fathers on those occasions. " Do not you think (says he) that the Lacedæmonians hate their children, who try their tempers by having them lashed publicly ? Their very fathers exhort them firmly to bear the lashes of the whips ; and intreat them, when torn to pieces and half dead, still to continue to offer their wounds to other wounds."

In fine, with so much solemnity were the flagellating ceremonies and trials we mention performed, that a priestess, as Silenus of Chios relates, constantly presided over them, holding up a small statue of the goddess in her hand while the young men were lashed ; and, to crown all, priests were established to inspect the stripes and marks of the blows, and draw omens from them.   "I am witness (says Lucian) that there are priests appointed to inspect the lashes and stripes."   To this it may be added, that these extraordinary ceremonies of the Lacedæmonians, which are here described, were preserved among them, notwithstanding the numerous revolutions which their republic underwent, to very late times ; and Tertullian mentions them as continuing, in his days, to be regularly celebrated every year. "For (says the author) the festival of the flagellations is still in these days looked upon as a very great solemnity at Lacedæmon. Everybody knows in what temple all the young men of the best families are lashed in the presence of their relations and friends, who exhort them to bear to the last this cruel ceremony."

Even philosophers among the Greeks, I mean particular sects of them, had adopted the practice of voluntary flagellation. Lucian relates in one of his dialogues, that there were philosophers in his time, "who trained young men to endure labour, pain, and want; and who made the practice of virtue consist in these austerities. A number of them would bind themselves; others whipped themselves; and those who were the most tender, flead their outer skin with instruments of iron made for that purpose."

However, austerities of this kind were only practiced by particular sects of philosophers, as hath been above observed; and the generality of them were so far from adopting such practices, that a great many ridiculed them. Of this we have an instance in the book of the Life of Apollonius Tyanæus, written by Philostrates. In this book, Apollonius is said to have spoken in the following manner to Thespesion. "Flagellations are practiced before the altar of Diana Scythia, because the oracles have ordered it so; now I think that it would be folly to resist the will of the gods. If so (Thespesion answers) you show, O Apollonius, that the gods of the Greeks possess but little wisdom, since they prescribe to men who think they are free to lash themselves with whips."

Nor was the practice of those flagellations to which the persons who underwent them willingly submitted, confined to the nations of Greece; but the same had also been adopted in other countries. It obtained among the Thracians, as we find in Artemidorus. "The young men of noble families among the Thracians (says the author) are on certain occasions cruelly lashed."

Voluntary Flagellations among the Egyptians, Syrians, and Romans.

Voluntary flagellations were also in use among the Egyptians. It even seems that this practice took its origin among them; and they used them as a method of atoning for their sins, and appeasing the incensed Deity. Herodotus has left us an account of the manner in which they commonly performed their flagellations, in the account he has given of the festival which they celebrated in honour of their goddess.   After preparing themselves by fasting (he says) they begin to offer sacrifices, and they mutually beat each other during the time that the offerings are burning on the altar; this done, the viands which remain after the sacrifice is accomplished, are placed upon tables before those who compose the assembly."

The same Herodotus says on another occasion, "I have already related in what manner the festival of Isis is celebrated in the city of Busiris.   While the sacrifice is performing, the whole assembly, amounting to several thousands of both men and women, beat one another."   To this Herodotus adds, that "he is not allowed to mention the reason, why those beatings were performed."

Among the Syrians, we likewise find that the use of voluntary flagellations had been adopted; and their priests practised them upon themselves with astonishing severity.   Apuleius, in his Metamorphosis of the Golden Ass, relates the manner in which these priests both made incisions in their own flesh, and lashed themselves voluntarily.

"In fine, they dissect their own arms with two-edged knives, which they use constantly to carry about them.   In the meanwhile, one of them begins to rave and sigh, and seems to draw his breath from his very bowels.   He at last feigns to fall into a kind of phrenetic fit, pretending that he is replete with the spirit of the goddess; as if the presence of the gods ought not to make man better, instead of rendering them disordered and weak.   But now, behold what kind of favour the Divine Will is going to bestow upon him.   He begins to vociferate, and, by purposely contrived lies, to upbraid and accuse himself in the same manner as if he had been guilty of having entertained bad designs against the mysteries of their holy religion. He then proceeds to award a sentence of punishment against himself; and at the same time grasping his scourge, an instrument which those priests constantly wear about them, and which is made of twisted woollen cords armed with small bones, he lashes himself with repeated blows; all the while manifesting a wonderful, though affected firmness, notwithstanding the violence and number of the stripes." From all that is above related, it is pretty evident that those Syrian priests used (or seemed to use) themselves in this cruel manner, only with a view to raise admiration in the minds of weak and superstitious persons by this extraordinary affectation of superior sanctity, and thereby to cheat them out of their money. At least this is the conjecture made by Philippus Beroaldus, in his commentaries on the Metamorphosis of the Golden Ass, who says, that those priests were no better than jugglers, or rather cheats, who only aimed at catching the money of the fools who gazed at them.

Nay, the opinion of the merit of voluntary or religious flagellations, was in ancient times grown so universal, that we find them to have also been practised among the Romans, who had adopted notions on that subject of the same kind with those of the Syrians and the Egyptians, and thought that the gods were, upon particular occasions, to be appeased by using scourges and whips. An instance of this notion or practice is to be met with in the Satyricon of Petronius, in which Encolpus relates, that, being upon the sea, the people of the ship flagellated him, in order as they thought to prevent a storm. "It was resolved (he says) among the mariners, to give us each forty stripes, in order to appease the tutelar deity of the ship. No time accordingly is lost; the furious mariners set upon us with cords in their hands, and endeavour to appease the deity by the effusion of the meanest blood: as for me, I received three lashes, which I endured with Spartan magnanimity."

But the most curious instance of religious flagellations among the Romans, and indeed among all other nations, is that of the ceremony which the Romans called Lupercalia; a ceremony which was performed in honour of the god Pan, and had been contrived in Arcadia, where it was in use so early as the times of king Evander, and whence it was afterwards brought over to Italy.   In this festival, a number of men used to dance naked, as Virgil informs us. "Here (says he) the dancing Salii, and naked Luperci." And Servius, in his commentary on this verse of Virgil, explains to us who these Luperci were.   "They were (he says) men, who upon particular solemnities, used to strip themselves stark naked; in this situation they ran about the streets, carrying straps of leather in their hands, with which they struck the women they met in their way. Nor did those women run away from them; on the contrary, they willingly presented the palms of their hands to them, in order to receive their blows, imagining, through a superstitious notion received among the Romans, that these blows, whether applied to their hands or to their belly, had the power of rendering them fruitful, or procuring them an easy delivery."

The same facts are also alluded to, by Juvenal, who says in his second satire, "Nor is it of any service to her, to offer the palms of her hands to a nimble Lupercus."   And the ancient scholiast on Juvenal observes on this verse, that barren women, in Rome, used to throw themselves into the way of the Luperci when become furious, and were beaten by them with straps.

Other authors, besides those above, have mentioned this festival of the Lupercalia.

Among others, Festus, in his book on the Signification of

Words, informs us, that the Luperci were also called Crepi, on account of the kind of noise *(crepitus)* which they made with their straps, when they struck the women with them ; " For it is a custom among the Romans (continues the same author) for men to run about naked during the festival of the Lupercalia, and to strike all the women they meet with straps."

Prudentius, I find, has also mentioned the same festival in his Roman Martyr : " what is the meaning (says he) of this shameful ceremony ? By thus running about the streets, under the shape of Luperci, you show that you are persons of low condition. Would you not deem a man to be the meanest of slaves, who would run naked about the public streets, and amuse himself with striking the young women ?

All the flagellations we have above mentioned were performed in public solemnities, or with religious views of some kind or other ; but there were other instances of voluntary flagellations (as we learn from the ancient authors) in which those who performed them were actuated by no such laudable motives ; or at least, had no precise intention that has been made known to us. Such were the flagellations mentioned by St. Jerom, in his observations on the epitaph of the widow Marcella. In these observations, St. Jerom informs us, that there were men in Rome silly enough to lay their posteriors bare in the public markets, or open streets, and to suffer themselves to be lashed by a pretended conjuror. " It is no wonder (says he) that a false diviner lashes the buttocks of those blockheads in the middle of the streets, and in the market-place."

And these conjurors not only lashed the persons who desired them to do so, but they, at other times, would also lash themselves, as we learn from Plautus, though an early writer ; for those flagellations we mention were, it seems, an old practice among the vulgar in Rome.   " Pray, is it not (says an actor in one of this author's plays) is it not the conjuror who lashes himself."

Another proof of the practice of those both active and passive flagellations which prevailed among the people in Rome, is also to be drawn from the above mentioned book of Festus, on the Signification of Words.   Festus, explaining in that book the signification of the word *Flagratores*, says, that this word signified "those who allowed themselves to be whipped for money."   And M. Dacier, a person of consummate learning in all that relates to antiquity, says in his notes on the above author, that the word *Flagratores*, signified likewise "those who whipped others," he adds, that this was the more common acceptation of the word.

Besides the flagellations just mentioned, which perhaps were also owing to some superstitious notion or other in those persons who practised them, we find, in ancient authors, instances of lashings and whippings performed in a way perfectly jocular, and as a kind of innocent pastime.   None is more remarkable than that which is related by Lucian of the philosopher Peregrinus.   This Peregrinus (Lucian observes) was a cynic philosopher of a very impudent disposition.   He lived in the time of the Emperor Trajan.   After having embraced the Christian religion, he returned to his former sect, and then used frequently to lash himself in public in rather an indecent manner. "Surrounded by a crowd of spectators, he handled his *pudendum* which he exhibited as a thing, he said, of no value.   He afterwards both gave himself and received from the bystanders, lashes upon his posteriors, and performed a number of other juvenile tricks equally surprising as these."

We also find in Suetonius another instance of sportive lashings or flappings among the ancients ; and these, too, practised upon no less a person than a Roman emperor.   The emperor here alluded to was the Emperor Claudius. "When he happened" says Suetonius, "to fall asleep after his dinner, which was a customary thing with him, they threw stones of olives or of dates at him in order to awaken him ; or sometimes the Court buffoons would rouse him by striking him, in a jocular way, with a strap or a scourge."

The following is an instance of voluntary flagellation among the ancients, which was not only free either from the superstition or wantonness above mentioned, but was moreover produced by rational, and, we may say, laudable motives. The instance referred to is that of the flagellations bestowed upon himself by a certain philosopher mentioned by Suidas. The philosopher's name was Superanus : he was a disciple of Lascaris. Though past the age of thirty years, he had taken a strong resolution of applying himself to science, and began at that time to read the works of the most famous orators. So earnest was he in his design of succeeding in those studies which he had undertaken, that "he never grudged himself either the rod or sharp lectures, in order to learn all that schoolmasters and tutors teach their pupils. He even was more than once seen, in the public baths, to inflict upon himself the severest corrections."

Chap. III.—*The practice of scourging one's self unknown to the early Christians.*

FLAGELLATIONS of different kinds being universally practised among the heathens, this circumstance must needs have given but little encouragement to the first Christians, to imitate such mode of correction; and we may take it for granted that they had not adopted it. Indeed, we find that no mention is made of it in the writings of the first, either Greek or Latin Fathers; for instance, in the Epistles of St. Ignatius, the Apologies of Justinius, the Apostolic Canons, the Constitutions attributed to Clement the Roman, the works of Origen, the *Stromats* of Clement of Alexandria, and all the works in general of Eusebius of Cæsarea, of St. Chrysostom, of St. Basil, and of St. Basil of Selucia. In all the above authors, no mention, I say, is made of flagellations; at least, of those of a voluntary kind; unless we are absolutely to explain in a literal manner, passages in which they manifestly spoke in a figurative sense. We may therefore safely conclude, that the first Christians had no notion of those cruel exercises which prevailed in later days, and that to flay one's hide with scourges or rods, as is in these times the practice of numberless devotees, in or out of religious orders, were practices unknown to them.

Regard for truth, however, obliges us to mention one or two instances of flagellations, which are to be found in the history of the ancient eastern Anchorites, written by Theodoret, who has been above mentioned; but those instances are such, that certainly no argument can be derived from them, to prove that voluntary flagellations were in use in the times in which those Anchorites lived.

One of those instances is to be found in the life of Abrahames. It is related in it, that the Christian populace having attempted to seize the sheets in which the body of that saint was wrapped, the lictors drove them back with whips. Now it is obvious to everyone, that the lashes which these lictors bestowed, to and fro and at random, upon those men who beset them, were not willingly received by the latter. And the same may certainly with equal truth be observed of the flagellations inflicted upon the people (which is the second instance mentioned by Theodoret) by the collectors of the public tributes, who, he says, used to collect them with scourges and whips.

The rules of the first religious orders founded in the west, have been likewise silent as to the voluntary use of thongs and whips. The first rule, for instance, prescribed to the Benedictines, that ancient western order, does not mention a word about self-flagellation; and the same silence is to be observed in the rules framed by Ovisiesius, Abbot of Tabennæ; by St. Aurelian, Bishop of Arles; by St. Isidorus, Bishop of Sevil; by St. Tetradius; and a number of others, whose rules Holstenius has likewise collected. From thence we may therefore conclude, that Christians in those times, had no notion of those beatings and scourgings which are now so prevalent, and that the upper and lower disciplines were alike unknown among them.

The only author of weight, in the days we speak of, who seems to have made any mention of voluntary flagellations being practised in the ancient monasteries, is St. John Climax, who according to some accounts, lived in the middle of the fourth, and according to others, only in the sixth century. This author relates, that, in a certain monastery, "some, among the monks, watered the pavement with their tears; while others, who could not shed any, beat themselves."

Flagellation Bestowed by the Devil.

To those instances of involuntary flagellations, during the times of the eastern Anchorites and the first monks, we may, I think, safely add those which the devil, jealous of their merit, has inflicted upon them; a case which has frequently happened, if we are to credit the writers of those times.

In the lives of the saints remarkable virtues are recited; whether it was that those saints, after having dreamed of such flagellations, fancied they had in reality received them, and spoke accordingly, or that they had some scheme in view when they made complaints of that kind. St. Francis of Assisa, for instance, as is related in the Golden Legend, received a dreadful flagellation from the devil the very first night he was in Rome, which caused him to leave that place without delay. And, to say the truth, it is not at all unlikely that, having met there with a colder reception than he judged his sanctity entitled him to, he thought proper to decamp immediately, and when he returned to his convent, told the above story to his monks.

Among those saints who received flagellations, or visits in general, from the devil, St. Anthony is however the most celebrated. At some times the devil, as is mentioned above, flagellated him vigorously; and at others, employed temptations of quite a different kind, in order to seduce him: thus, he assumed in one instance the shape of a beautiful young woman, who made all imaginable advances to the saint; but, happily, all was to no purpose. The celebrated engraver, Callot, has made one of those visits of the devil to St. Anthony, the subject of one of his prints, which is inscribed the Temptation of St. Anthony; and he has represented in it such a numerous swarm of devils of all sizes, pouring at once into the saint's cavern, and exhibiting so surprising a variety of faces, postures, and ludicrous weapons, such as squirts, bellows, and the like, that this print may very well be mentioned as an instance, among others, of the great fertility of the imagination of that engraver.

Besides the persecutions which St. Anthony suffered from the devil, he has the farther merit of having been the first institutor of the monastic life, several other hermits having in his time chosen to assemble together, and lived under his direction ; and though he has not expressly been the founder of any particular order, yet it is glory enough for him to have been the father of the whole family of friars and nuns. In more modern times, however, his relics having been brought from Egypt to Constantinople, and thence transferred to Dauphine, in France, a church was built on the spot where they were deposited, and a new order of friars was a little after established, who go by the name of Monks of St. Anthony. These monks form a kind of order distinct from all others ; but yet they have no less ingenuity than the other monks for procuring the good of their convent, as may be judged from the following story, which, I think, I may venture to relate as a conclusion of the chapter.

The story I mean, is contained in the book of the *Apologie pour Herodote*, which was written about the year 1500 by Henry Etienne, on purpose to show that those who entirely reject the facts related by Herodotus, on account of their incredibility, treat them with too much severity, since a number of facts daily happen which are altogether as surprising as those that are found in that author.

Before relating the story in question, the reader ought to be informed, that St. Anthony is commonly thought to have a great command over fire, and a power of destroying, by flashes of that element, those who incur his displeasure. The common people have been led into this belief, by constantly seeing a fire placed by the side of that saint in the representations that are made of him; though this fire is placed there for no other reason than because the saint is thought to have the power of curing the erysipelas, which is also called the sacred fire *(ignis facer)*, in the same manner as St. Hubert cures the hydrophoby; St. John, the epilepsy; and other saints, other disorders. A certain monk of St. Anthony (to come to our point) who was well acquainted with the above prepossession of the vulgar concerning his saint, used on Sundays to preach in public, in different villages within a certain distance from his convent. One day he assembled his congregation under a tree on which a magpie had built her nest, into which he had previously found means to convey a small box filled with gunpowder, which he had well secured therein; and out of the box hung a long thin match, that was to burn slowly, and was hidden among the leaves of the tree. As soon as the monk, or his assistant, had touched the match with a lighted coal, he began his sermon. In the meanwhile the magpie returned to her nest; and finding in it a strange body which she could not remove, she fell into a passion, and began to scratch with her feet, and chatter unmercifully. The friar affected to hear her without emotion and continued his sermon with great composure; only he would now and then lift up his eyes towards the top of the tree, as if he wanted to see what was the matter. At last, when he judged the fire was very near reaching the gunpowder, he pretended to be quite out of patience, he cursed the magpie, and wished St. Anthony's fire might consume her, and went on again with his sermon; but he had scarcely pronounced a few periods, when the match on a sudden produced its effect, and blew up the magpie with her nest; which miracle wonderfully raised the character of the friar, and proved afterwards very beneficial both to him and his convent.

Chap. IV.—*Corrections of a flagellatory kind, inflicted by force;
the common method of correcting offences of a religious nature;
and the power of inflicting them possessed alike by Bishops
and the heads of Monasteries.*

IT must be confessed, however, that though self-flagellation
made no part of the rules or statutes belonging to the
different monastic orders, founded ·in those early stages of
Christianity, the same cannot be said of that method of correction,
when imposed by force upon such monks as had been guilty of
offences, either against the discipline of the order, or against
piety : an extensive power of inflicting such salutary corrections,
having, from the earliest times, been lodged in the hands of abbots
and the superiors of convents.

Nay more, we find that bishops during the very first times of
Christianity, assumed the paternal power we mention, even with
regard to persons who were bound to them by no vow whatever,
when they happened to have been guilty either of breaches of
piety or of heresy. Of this, a remarkable proof may be deduced
from the 59th Epistle of St. Augustin, which he wrote to the
Tribune Marcellinus, concerning the Donatists. St. Augustin
expresses himself in the following words : " Do not recede from
that parental diligence you have manifested in your researches
after offenders ; in which you have succeeded to procure con-
fessions of such great crimes, not by using racks, red-hot blades
of iron, or flames, but only by the application of rods. This is a
method of coercion which is frequently practised by teachers of
the fine arts upon their pupils, by parents upon their children,
and often also by bishops upon those whom they find to have been
guilty of offences."

Another proof of this power of flagellation, assumed by bishops in very early times, may be derived from the account which Cyprianus has given of Cesarius, Bishop of Arles; who says, that that bishop endeavoured as much as possible, in the exercise of his power, to keep within the bounds of moderation prescribed by the law of Moses. The following are Cyprianus's words: "This holy man took constant care that those who were subjected to his authority, whether they were of a free or servile condition, when they were to be flagellated for some offence they had committed, should not receive more than thirty-nine stripes. If any of them, however, had been guilty of a previous fault, then indeed he permitted them to be again lashed a few days afterwards, though with a smaller number of stripes."

From the two passages above, we are informed that the power of whipping, possesed by bishops, extended to persons of every vocation, indiscriminately; and with much more reason may we think that those persons who made profession of the ecclesiastical life, were subjected to it. In fact we see that even the different dignities which they might possess in the church, did not exempt them from having a flagellation inflicted upon them by their bishops, when they had been guilty of offences of rather a serious kind; and Pope St. Gregory the Great, moreover, recommended to the bishops of his time, to make a proper use of their authority. In his sixty-sixth Epistle, he himself prescribes to Bishop Paschasius, the manner in which he ought to chastise Deacon Hilary who had caluminated Deacon John. "Whereas" he says, "guilt ought not to pass without adequate satisfaction, we recommend to Bishop Paschasius to deprive the same Deacon Hilary of his office, and after having caused him to be publicly lashed, to confine him to some distant place; that the punishment inflicted upon one, may thus serve to the correction of many."

This power of inflicting the brotherly correction of whipping was also possessed by the abbots and priors in all the ancient monasteries; though, at the same time, it was expressly provided by the rules of the different orders, that the same should be assumed by no other persons. "Let no man, except the abbot or him to whom he has intrusted his authority, presume to excommunicate, or flog a brother."

When the faults committed by monks were of a grevious kind, the abbot was not only charged to correct them by means of his discretionery power of flagellation, but he was moreover expressly directed to exert that power with rigour. In the rule framed by St. Fructuosus, Bishop of Braga, it is ordained with respect to a monk who is convicted of being a liar, a thief, or a striker, "That if, after being warned by the elder monks he neglects to mend his manners, he shall, on the third time, be exhorted in the presence of all the brethren, to leave off his bad practices. If he still neglects to reform, let him be flagellated with the utmost severity." The above rule of St. Fructuosus is mentioned by Ecbert, in his Collection of Canons, which together with his Councils of England, has been published by Spelman.

St. Ferreol, Bishop of Usez, framed a rule for monks, which like that above, makes severe provisions against such monks as are addicted to the practice of thieving. "With regard to the monk who stands convicted of theft, if we may still call him a monk, he shall be treated like him who is guilty of adultery for the second time; let him therefore be chastised with the whip, and with great rigour too. The same punishment ought to be inflicted upon him as upon a fornicator, since it may be justly suspected that his lewdness has induced him to commit theft."

Committing indecencies with other monks, or with boys, were offences which the Statutes of Convents likewise directed to be punished by severe flagellations; and the above St. Fructuosus, Bishop of Braga, ordered that the punishment should, in the above case, be inflicted publicly. "If a monk" it is said in his rule, "is used to tease boys and young men, or is caught in attempting to give them kisses, or in any other indecent action, and the fact be proved by competent witnesses, let him be publicly whipped."

Refusing to make proper satisfaction to the abbot for offences committed, or in general persevering in denying them, were also grevious faults in the eye of the first founders, or reformers, of monastic orders. In the rule framed fifty years after that of St. Benedict, in order to improve it, the following direction was contained : "If the brothers who have been excommunicated for their faults, persevere so far in their pride, as to continue, on the ninth hour of the next day, to refuse to make proper satisfaction to the abbot, let them be confined, even till their death, and lashed with rods." Nor is the rule of the above-mentioned Bishop of Braga less severe against those monks whose pride prevents them from making a proper confession of the offences they may have committed. "To him" it is said in that rule, "who, through pride and inclination to argue, continues to deny his fault, let an additional and severer flagellation be imparted."

The habit of holding wanton discourses, or soliciting the brethren to wickedness, was also deemed by the founders of religious orders to deserve severe flagellations ; and St. Pacom ordered in his rule, which it was said had been dictated to him by an angel, that such as had been guilty of the above faults, and had been thrice admonished, should be publicly lashed before the gate of the convent.

Attempts to escape from monasteries, were, even in very early times, punished by flagellation. We read in Sozomenius, that St. Macarius of Alexandria, Abbot of Nitria in Thebaid, who had five thousand monks under his direction, ordered that chastisement to be inflicted upon those who should attempt to climb over the walls of the monasteries. "If anyone continues in his wickedness, and says, I can no longer bear to stay here, but I will pack up my things and go where God will direct me; let any one of the brothers inform the prior, and the prior the abbot, of the fact; let then the abbot assemble the brothers, and order the offender to be brought before them and chastised with rods."

The holy founders of religious orders have also been very severe, in their provisions, against such monks as seek for familiarities with the other sex. In the rule of the Monastery of Agaunus, it was ordained, that, "If any monk had contracted the bad habit of looking on women with concupiscence, the abbot ought to be informed of the fact, and bestow upon the monk a corrective discipline; and that, if he did not mend his manners in consequence thereof, he ought to be expelled from the society as a scabby sheep, lest he should ruin others by his example." The above monastery had been built by Sigismond, King of Burgundy, to the honour of one hundred and twenty Martyrs of the Theban Legion, of which St. Maurice was the commander, under the reign of the Emperor Maximinus.

The above-quoted rule of St. Fructuosus, is no less severe against those monks who seek for the company of women. In the fifteenth chapter, which treats of the lewd and quarrelsome, it is ordered, that, "if after having received proper reprehensions they persist in their wicked courses, they shall be corrected by repeated lashings." And St. Columbanus, who is the first who instituted the monastic life in France, and has written a rule as a supplement to that of St. Benedict, also expresses himself with great severity against such monks as are convicted of having barely conversed with a woman in the absence of witnesses; for though there are faults for which he orders only six lashes to be given, yet, in the case here mentioned he prescribes two hundred. "Let the man who has been alone with a woman, and talked familiarly to her, either be kept on bread and water for two days, or receive two hundred lashes."

THE holy founders of religious orders considered flagellations as being less useful in the convents of women, than in those of men; and in the rules they have framed for them, they have accordingly ordered that kind of correction to be inflicted upon those whose bad conduct made it necessary.

This chastisement of flagellation, upon women who make a profession of a religious life, is no new thing in the world. It was the chastisement appropriated to the vestals, in antient Rome; and we find in the historians, that when faults had been committed by them in the discharge of their functions, it was commonly inflicted upon them by the hands of the priests, or sometimes of the great priest himself.

Dionysius of Halicarnassus relates, that the virgin Urbinia was lashed by the priests, and led in procession through the town.

The high priest, Publius Licinius, ordered, as we read in Valerius Maximus, "that a certain vestal who had suffered the sacred fire to be extinguished, should be lashed and dismissed."

Julius likewise relates, "that the fire in the Temple of Vesta having happened to be extinguished, the virgin was whipped by the high priest, M. Æmilus, and promised never to offend again in the same manner." And Festus says in his book, that "whenever the fire of Vesta came to be extinguished, the virgins were lashed by the great priest."

Severities of the like kind have been deemed necessary to be introduced into the convents of modern nuns, by the holy fathers who have framed religious rules for them.

In that very ancient rule for the conduct of nuns, which is contained in epistle cix. of St. Augustin, the mortification of discipline is prescribed to the prioress herself. "Let her" it is said in the above rule, "be ever ready to receive discipline, but never impose it but with fear."*

Cesarius, Archbishop of Arles, in the rule framed by him which is mentioned with praise by several ancient authors, such, as Genadius, and Gregory of Tours, prescribes the discipline of flagellation to be inflicted upon nuns who have been guilty of faults; and enters, besides, into several particulars about the propriety as well as usefulness of this method of correction. "It is just" he says, "that such as have violated the institutions contained in the rule should receive an adequate discipline; it is fit that in them should be accomplished what the Holy Ghost has in former times prescribed through Solomon: He who loves his child, frequently applies the rod to it."

St. Donat, Archbishop of Bezancon, in the rule he has framed for nuns, has expressed the same paternal disposition towards them as Archbishop Cesarius has done: he recommends flagellations as excellent methods of mending the morals of such of them as are wickedly inclined, or careless in performing their religious duties; and he determines the different kinds of faults for which the above correction ought to be bestowed upon them, as well as the number of the blows that are to be inflicted. The above rule of St. Donat has been mentioned with much praise by the Monk Jonas, in his account of the life of St. Columbanus, which the venerable Beda has inserted in the third volume of his works.

---

* Num. xii. "Disciplinam lubens habeat, metuens imponat."

In that rule, commonly called the rule of a father, which St
Benedict, Bishop of Aniana, in his book on the concordance of
rules, and Smaragdus in his commentaries on the rule of St Benedict, have both mentioned, provisions of the same kind as those
are made for the correction of nuns. "If a sister" it is said in
that rule, "that has been several times admonished, will not
mend her conduct, let her be excommunicated for a while in proportion to the degree of her fault; if this kind of correction proves
useless, let her then be chastised by stripes."

Striking a sister has likewise been looked upon as an offence
of a grevious kind; and St. Aurelian, in the rule he has framed
for nuns, orders a discipline to be inflicted on such as have been
guilty of it.

To the above regulations, Archbishop Cesarius has added
another, which is, that the corrections ought for the sake of
example to be inflicted in the presence of all the sisters. "Let
also the discipline be bestowed upon them in the presence of the
congregation, conformable to the precepts of the apostle. Confute
sinners in the presence of all."

The Methods of Self Mortification as appears to have been Practised in Early Times.

It is expressly said of St. Pardulph, a Benedictine Monk and
Abbot, who lived during the time of Charles Martel, about the
year 737, that he used in Lent-time to strip himself stark naked,
and order one of his disciples to lash him. The fact is related in
the life of that saint, formerly written by an author who lived
about the same time; and it was, two hundred years afterwards,
put into more elegant language by Yvus, Prior of Clugny, at the
desire of monks of St. Martial, in the town of Limoges. Hugh
Menard, a Benedictine Father, and a very learned man in all
that relates to ecclesiastical antiquities, has inserted part of it in

his book, intitled, "Observations on the Benedictine Martyrology." The following is the passage in St. Pardulph's Life, which is here alluded to.   "St. Pardulph seldom went out of his cell; whenever sickness obliged him to bathe, he would previously make incisions in his own skin.   During Lent he used to strip himself entirely naked, and ordered one of his disciples to lash him with rods."

St. William, Duke of Aquitain, who lived in the time of Charlemagne, that is about the year 800, and many years before Cardinal Damian; is said to have also used flagellations, as a means of voluntary penance.   Arduinus, the writer of the holy duke's life, and a contemporary writer, says, that "it was commonly reported that the duke did frequently, for the love of Christ, cause himself to be whipped, and that he then was alone with the person who assisted him."   Haeftenus, Superior of the Monastery of Affigen, relates the same fact, and says that the Duke of Aquitain "took a great delight in sleeping upon a hard bed, and that he moreover lashed himself with a scourge."   Hugh Menard, the learned Benedictine just now mentioned, has adopted the testimony of Arduinus, and upon that writer's authority inserted the above fact in his "Observations on the Benedictine Martyrology."

Other persons, who lived before the times of Cardinal Damian, are also mentioned by different writers as having practised voluntary flagellations.   Gaulbertus, Abbot of Pontoise, who lived about the year 900, upon a certain occasion, "severely flagellated himself (as M. Du Cange relates in his glossary) with a scourge made of knotted thongs."   And the above-mentioned Haeftenus, Prior of Affigen, has advanced that the same practice was followed by St. Romuald, who lived about the same time as Gualbertus, and by the monks of the Camaldolian order, who were settled in Sitria.

Another early instance of voluntary flagellations occurs in the life of Guy, Abbot of Pomposa. Heribert, it is said, Archbishop of Ravenna, formed the design of pulling down the Monastery of Pomposo; and this piece of news caused both Abbot Guy and his monks "to lock themselves up in the capitular house, and to lash themselves every day, for several days, with rods." Abbot Guy was born in the year 956; and he was made Abbot of Pomposa in the year 998, in which capacity he continued forty-eight years.

All the facts above related were anterior to the year 1056, the time at which Peter Damian de Honestis was raised to the Cardinalship by Pope Stephen IX; and it is evident from them, that the practice of voluntarily flagellating oneself as a penance for committed sins, had been adopted before the period in question, though it cannot be said to have been then universally prevalent; at least only a few instances of it have been left us by the writers of those times. But at the era we mention, this pious mode of self correction, owing to the public and zealous patronage with which the above Cardinal favoured it, acquired a vast degree of credit and grew into universal esteem; and then it was that persons of religious dispositions were everywhere seen to arm themselves with whips, rods, thongs, and besoms, and lacerate their own hides, in order to draw upon themselves the favour of heaven.

We are informed of this fact by the learned Cardinal Baronius, in his Ecclesiastical Annals. "At that time" he says, "the laudable usage of the faithful of beating themselves with whips made for that purpose, though Peter Damian may not be said to have been the author of it, was much promoted by him in the christian church; in which he followed the example of the blessed Dominic the Cuirassed, a holy hermit, who had subjected himself to his authority."

The same Cardinal Damian has moreover left numerous accounts of voluntary flagellations practised by certain holy men of his times; but these are surely more apt to create our admiration, than to excite us to imitate them. Indeed the flagellations he mentions cannot be proposed to the faithful as examples they ought to follow; and they were executed with such dreadful severity, as makes it impossible for the most vigorous men to go through the like, without a kind of miracle.

In the Life of the Monk St. Rodolph, who was afterwards made Bishop Eugubio, the Cardinal relates, "That this holy man would often impose upon himself a penance of an hundred years, and that he performed it in twenty days, by the strenuous application of a broom, without neglecting the other common methods used in doing penance. Every day, being shut up in his cell, he recited the whole psalter (or book of psalms) at least one time when he could not two, being all the while armed with a besom in each hand, with which he incessantly lashed himself."

The account which the Cardinal has left of Dominic, surnamed the Cuirassed, is not less wonderful. "His constant practice" he says, "is, after stripping himself naked, to fill both his hands with rods and then vigorously flagellate himself; this he does in his times of relaxation. But during Lent-time, or when he really means to mortify himself, he frequently undertakes the hundred years' penance; and then he every day recites the psalter at least three times over, all the while flogging himself with besoms."

Cardinal Damian then proceeds to relate the manner in which the same Dominic informed him he performed the hundred years' penance. "A man" said he, "may depend he has accomplished it, when he has flagellated himself during the whole time the psalter was sung twenty times over." The same author adds several circumstances which make the penances performed by the holy man appear in a still more admirable light. He, in the first place, was so dexterous as to be able to use both his hands at once, and thus laid on twice the number of lashes others could do who only used their right hand. In one instance he fustigated himself during the time the whole book of psalms was sung twice over; on another occasion he did the same while it was sung eight times; and on another, while it was repeated twelve times over; "which filled me with terror" the Cardinal adds, "when I heard the fact."

Cardinal Damian also relates of the same Dominic the Cuirassed, that he at last changed his discipline of rods into that of leather thongs, which was still harsher; and that he had been able to accustom himself to that laborious exercise. Nay, so punctual was he in performing the duties he had imposed upon himself, that, "when he happened to go abroad (being an hermit) he carried his scourge in his bosom, to the end that wherever he happened to spend the night, he might lose no time, and flog himself with the same regularity as usual. If the place in which he had taken his refuge for the night did not allow him to strip entirely, and fustigate himself from head to foot, he at least would severely beat his legs and head."

FLAGELLATION OF SOVERIGNS AND GREAT MEN.

Even sovereigns and great men, in the times we speak of, adopted for themselves the practice of voluntary flagellation.

The Emperor Henry, who lived about the year 1070, "never ventured (if we may credit Reginard's account) to put on his imperial robes, before he had obtained the permission of a priest for that purpose, and had deserved it by confession and discipline."

William of Nangis, in the Life of St. Lewis, King of France, which he has written, relates that that prince, after he had made his confession, constantly received discipline from his confessor.

To this the same author adds the following curious account: "I ought not to omit to say, concerning the confessor the king had before Geoffrey de Belloloco, and who belonged to the order of the Predicant Friars, that used to inflict upon him hard and immoderate disciplines; which the king, whose skin was rather tender, had much ado to endure. This hardship, however, he never would speak of to this confessor; but after his death, he mentioned the fact somewhat jocularly, though not without humility, to the new confessor."

An instance of much the same uature with the facts above recited, is to be found in one of Osbertus's books. A certain English count having contracted an unlawful marriage with one of his near relations, not only parted afterwards with her, but requested besides to be disciplined in the presence of St. Dunstan, and of the general assembly of the clergy. "Terrified" says Osbertus, "by the greatness of his offence, his obstinacy ceased; and after having renounced his unlawful wedlock, he imposed upon himself the task of penitence. As Dunstan was then presiding over a meeting of the clergy of the kingdom, which was holden according to custom, the count came into the middle of the assembly, barefooted, clothed with wool, and carrying rods in his hands; and threw himself, groaning and weeping, at the feet of St. Dunstan. This instance of piety moved the whole assembly, and Dunstan more than the rest. However, as his wish was thoroughly to reconcile the man with God, he preserved an appearance of severity in his looks, suitable to the occasion, and for a whole hour persevered in denying his request: when, at last, all the prelates having joined in the entreaties of the count, St. Dunstan granted him the indulgence he was suing for." From the above fact, we might conclude that flagellations voluntarily submitted to, had become, even before the era of Cardinal Damian, a settled method of atoning for past sins, since St.

Dunstan lived about an hundred years before the Cardinal; that is about the year 950.

Instances of sovereigns and great men requesting to undergo flagellations, must have been pretty common in the days we mention, frequent allusions being made to it in old books; among others in that old French romance, entitled, The History of the Round Table and the Feats of the Knight, Launcelot du Lac. King Arthur is supposed in it, to have summoned all the bishops who were in his army, to his chapel; and there to have requested of them, a correction of the same kind as that undergone by the count mentioned by Osbertus.

From the times we mention, we find numerous proofs of self-flagellation being used in convents : and indeed it would have been a very extraordinary circumstance if, while the persons above-named adopted that practice, monks had rejected it. In the fifty-third article of the statutes of the Abbey of Cluny, which were collected by Peter Maurice, surnamed the Venerable, who was raised to the dignity of Abbot in the year 1122, the following account is given. "It was ordained (it is said in that Article) that that part of the Monastery which is on the left, beyond the left Choir, should remain open to no strange persons, whether Ecclesiastical or Lay, as it was formerly, and nobody admitted into it except the Monks. This was thus settled, because the Brothers had no place, except the old Church of St. Peter, in which they could practise such holy and secret exercises as are usual with religious persons; they therefore claimed the use of the above new part of the Church, both for the night and the day, that they might constantly therein make offerings of the perfumes of their prayers to God, supplicate their Creator by frequent acts of repentance and genuflexions, and mortify their bodies by often inflicting upon themselves three flagellations, either as penances for their sins or as *an increase of their merit.*"

The practice in question gained so much credit, about those times, in Monasteries, that St. Bruno, who, a few years after the death of Cardinal Damian, founded the Carthusian Order, thought it necessary to restrain his Monks in that respect; not uulikely, perhaps, with the view to check the pride which they used to derive from such exercises. In one of the statutes laid by that Saint, which Prior Guiges has collected, the following regulation is contained. "In regard to such disciplines, watchings, and other religious exercises as are not expressly enjoined by our Institution, let nobody among us perform them, except it be by the Prior's permission."

LADY FLAGELLANTS.

So much were flagellations grown into fashion in the days we mention, such attractions did they even seem to possess, that ladies of high rank would also enlist among the above-mentioned Whippers, and almost vied with Dominic the Cuirassed, Rodolph de Eugubio, St. Anthelm, and Abbot Poppo, in regard to the regularity with which they performed such meritorious exercises. Among those ladies, particular mention is made of St. Maria of Ognia, of St. Hardwigge, Duchess of Poland, of St. Hildegarde, and above all of the Widow Cechald, who lived in the very times of Cardinal Damian, and performed wonderful feats in the same career, as we are informed by St. Antonius, upon the authority of Cardinal Damian himself. "Not only Men, but also Women of noble birth eagerly sought after that kind of purgatory; and the Widow of Cechaldus, a Woman of great birth and dignity, gave an account, that in consequeuce of an obligation she had previously imposed upon herself, she had gone through the hundred years' penance, three thousand lashes being the number allotted for every year."

The Widow Cechald, in her own account of the wonderful

penance she performed after the example of Dominic the *Cuir-assed*, has neglected to inform us in what manner she performed it, and whether she imitated that holy Man in every respect, and used, for instance, both her hands at once in the operation. Be it as it may, three hundred thousand lashes, the total amount of the hundred years' penance she went through, were certainly a very hard penance. However, as we are not to doubt either the account which the above Widow gave in that respect, or the declaration Cardinal Damian made after her, the wonder is to be explained another way, and perhaps by the nature of the instruments she made use of : they possibly were of much the same kind as those used by a certain lady, who was likewise much celebrated on account of the frequent disciplines she bestowed upon herself, and who was at last found out to use no other weapons for performing them than a bunch of feathers, or, as others have said, a fox's tail.

Chap. VI.—*Confessors assume to themselves a kind of flagellatory power over their Penitents.*

THE submission of sovereigns to receive disciplines from the hands of their confessors, together with the accounts of such disciplines, which, though they might not always be true, were industriously circulated in public, helped much, without doubt, to increase the good opinion which people entertained of the merit of flagellations, as well as to strengthen the power of confessors in general. In fact the latter, from prescribing disciplines, soon passed to inflicting them upon their penitents with their own hands; and without loss of time converted this newly-assumed authority into an express kind privilege, to which it was a most meritorious act, on the part of penitents, readily to submit. On this occasion I shall again quote the old French book previously mentioned, which, though it be only a romance, may serve to show the opinions generally entertained by people during the times in which it was written. "If you are estranged from our Lord's love, you cannot be reconciled to him, unless by the three following means: first, by confession of mouth; secondly, by a contrition of heart; thirdly, by works of alms and charity. Now go and make a confession in that manner, and receive discipline from the hands of thy confessors; for it is the sign of merit."

The power of confessors of disciplining their penitents, became in process of time so generally acknowledged, that it obtained even with respect to persons who made profession of the ecclesiastical life, and superseded the laws that had been made against those who should strike an ecclesiastic. To this an allusion is made in the lines of that poet of the middle age, who has put the *summula* of St. Raymund into Latin verses. "You are guilty of sacrilege if you have violated holy things, if you have struck a person in religious orders, or of the clergy; unless it be a holy beating, such as is performed by a teacher with respect to his disciple, or a confessor with respect to a person who confesses his sins."

Attempts were, however, made to put a stop to these practices of priests and confessors; and so early as under Pope Adrian I. who was raised to the purple in the year 772 (which by the by shows that the power assumed by confessors was pretty ancient) a regulation was made to forbid confessors to beat their penitents. "The bishop, (it is said in the Epitome of Maxims and Canons) the priest, and the deacon, must not beat those who have sinned." But this regulation proved useless: the whole tribe of priests, as well as the first dignitaries of the church, nevertheless continued to preach up the prerogatives of confessors and the merit of flagellations; and Cardinal Pullus, that chancellor of the Roman church who has been mentioned in the foregoing chapter, did not scruple to declare, that the nakedness of the penitent, and his situation at the feet of his confessor, were additional merits in him in the eye of God, as being additional tokens of his humility.

All these different practices of stripping and flagellating devotees and penitents at length gave rise to abuses of a very serious nature, instances of which took place, we may say, every day. Numbers of confessors, in process of time, have made such religious acts as had been introduced with a view to mortfication, serve to gratify their own lust and wantonness. They have tried to inculcate the same notions, as to the merit of flagellations, into the minds of their devotees of the other sex, as they had brought even kings and princes to entertain; and at last have made it a practice to inflict such corrections on their female penitents, and under that pretence to take such liberties with them, as the blessed St. Benedict, St. Francis, St. Dominic, and St. Loyola, had not certainly given them the example of.

Among the many instances that might be recited of the abuses here alluded to, it will suffice to produce that of a man who wore a hood, and was girt with a cord (a Cordelier or Franciscan) who lived about the year 1566. This man's name was Cornelius Adriasem; he was a native of Dort, and belonged to a convent in Bruges, and was a most violent preacher against the heretics, called Gueux. He had found means to persuade a certain number of women, both married and unmarried, to promise him implicit obedience, by certain oaths he made them take for that purpose, and under the specious pretence of greater piety. These women he did not indeed lash with harsh and knotted cords, but he used gently to rub their bare thighs and posteriors with willow or birch rods.

In order to show how common the above practices were become, as well as to entertain the reader, I give the following story, which is to be found in Scot's book, entitled, " Mensa Philosophica." " A woman," says Scot, " who was gone to make her confession, had been secretly followed by her husband, who was jealous of her, and he laid himself in some place in the church, whence he might spy her ; but as soon as he saw her led behind the altar by the priest in order to be flagellated, he made his appearance, objected that she was too tender to bear a flagellation, and offered to receive it in her stead. This proposal the wife greatly applauded, and the man had no sooner placed himself upon his knees than she exclaimed, ' Now, my father, lay on lustily, for I am a great sinner.' "

Cᴀᴅɪᴇʀᴇ Cᴀsᴇ.

A character who made some noise in the world was the celebrated Jesuit, Father Girard, and among the number of his pupils or penitents was Miss Cadiere, who certainly may also be looked upon as an illustrious character. The Cornelian disciplines which the Father used to serve upon her, were one of the subjects of the public complaint she afterwards preferred against him about the year 1730, which gave rise to a criminal lawsuit or prosecution that made a prodigious noise. It was thought to be a kind of stroke levelled at the whole Society of the Jesuits, and was known to have been stirred up by monks belonging orders who were at open emnity with them. The Demoiselle Cadiere likewise brought against Father Girard a charge of sorcery, and of having bewitched her ; in order, no doubt, to apologise for her having peaceably submitted to the licentious actions of which she accused the Father, as well as to those disciplines with which she reproached him, which she circumstantially described in the original complaint, or charge, which she preferred against him ; for judges are persons who will not understand things by half words,—one must speak plain to them, and call everything by its proper name. Father Girard, as is evident from the whole tenor of the declara, tion of Miss Cadiere herself, had as little intention as Abelard to do any injury to his pupil or penitent.

It must be observed that after all, confessors are nothing but men, and they are, under such circumstances, frequently agitated by thoughts not very consonant with the apparent gravity and sanctity of their looks. Nay, raising such thoughts in them, and in general creating sentiments of love in their confessors, are designs which numbers of female penitents—who at no time entirely cease being actuated by womanish views—expressly entertain, notwithstanding the apparent ingenuity of their confessions-

and in which they but too often succeed, to their own and their frail confessors' cost. Thus, it appears from Miss Cadiere's declarations, that she had of herself aimed at making the conquest of Father Girard, though a man past fifty years of age, being induced to it by his great reputation as a preacher and a man of parts ; and she expressly confessed that she had for a long while been making interest to be admitted into the number of his penitents.

ZACHARY CROFTON.

Among those who have distinguished themselves in the same career of flagellation was the Reverend Zachary Crofton, Curate of St. Botolph's, Aldgate, who, on a certain occasion, served a Cornelian discipline upon his chambermaid, for which she afterwards sued him at Westminster.

The aforesaid Zachary Crofton, as Bishop Kennet relates in his Chronicle from Dr. Calamy's notes, was formerly a Curate at Wrenbury, in Cheshire (it was a little before the Restoration), and he used to engage with much warmth in the religious and political quarrels of his times. His refusal to take the engagement, and dissuade others from taking it, caused him to be dismissed from his place. He was, however, afterwards provided with the curacy of St. Botolph's, Aldgate ; but as his turn for religious and political quarrels still prevailed, and he had written several pamphlets, both English and Latin, about the affairs of those times, he was sent to the Tower and deprived of his curacy. He was afterwards cast into prison likewise in his own county, and when he procured his liberty set up a grocer's shop. While he was in the above parish of St. Botolph, "he gave," as Dr. Calamy relates, "the correction of a school boy to his servant-maid," for which she prosecuted him in Westminster Hall. This fact the Doctor relates as an instance of the many scrapes into which Zachary Crofton's warm and zealous temper brought him ;

and he adds that on the last mentioned occasion, "he was bold to print his defence." Indeed, this fact of Parson Crofton's undauntedly appealing to the public in print concerning the lawfulness of the flagellation he had performed, places him, notwithstanding what Dr. Calamy may add as to the mediocrity of his parts, at least upon a level with the geniuses above mentioned, as well as any other of the kind that may be named, and cannot fail for ever to secure him a place among the most illustrious flagellators.

In fine, to this list of the persons who have distinguished themselves by the flagellations they have achieved, I think I cannot avoid adding the lady mentioned by Brantôme, who (perhaps as an exercise conducive to her health) took great delight in performing corrections of this kind with her own hands. This lady, who was moreover a very great lady, would often, as Brantôme relates, cause the ladies of her household to strip themselves, and then amuse herself in giving them slaps pretty lustily laid on. With respect to those ladies who had committed faults, she made use of good rods ; and in general, she used less or greater severity, according (Brantôme says) as she proposed to make them either laugh or cry.

CHAP. VII.—*The Church at large claims the power of publicly inflicting the discipline of Flagellation. Instances of Kings and Princes who have submitted to it.*

AS it was the constant practice of Priests and Confessors to prescribe Flagellation as a part of the *satisfaction* that was owing for committed sins, the opinion came at last to be established that receiving this kind of correction was not only a useful but even an indispensable act of submission : without it, penitence was thought to be a body without a soul, nor could there be any such thing as true repentance. Hence the Church itself at large came also in time to claim a power of imposing castigations of the kind we mention upon naked sinners ; and a flagellation publicly submitted to has been made one of the essential ceremonies to be gone through, for obtaining the inestimable advantage of the repeal of a sentence of excommunication: the Roman Ritual expressly mentioning and requiring this test of the culprit's contrition.

These flagellatory claims and practices of the Western Christian Church, are, we may observe, one of the objections made against it by the Greek, or Eastern Christians, as the learned M. Cotelier, a Doctor of the Sorbonne, observes in his *Monuments of the Greek Church:* "When they absolve a person from his excommunication (they say) he is stripped down to the waist, and they lash him with a scourge on that part which is bare, and then absolve him, as being forgiven his sin."

Among the different instances of disciplines publicly inflicted by the Church upon independent Princes, we may mention that which was imposed upon Giles, Count of the Venaissin County, near Avignon. This Count having caused the Curate of a certain parish to be buried alive, who had refused to bury the body of a poor man till the usual fees were paid, drew upon himself the wrath of the Pope, who fulminated against him a sentence of excommunication.   And in order to procure the repeal of it, he found it necessary to submit to a flagellation, which was inflicted upon him before the gate of the Cathedral Church of Avignon.

But no fact can be mentioned more striking, and more capable of having gratified the pride of the Clergy, at the time, than that of Henry II., King of England.   This Prince having, by a few hasty, angry words he uttered on a certain occasion, been the cause of the assassination of Thomas Becket, Archbishop of Canterbury, expressed afterwards the greatest sorrow for his imprudence : but neither the priests nor the nation would take his word on that account : they only gave credit to the reality of his repentance, when he had submitted to the all-purifying trial of a flagellation ; and in order the more completely to remove all doubts in that respect he went through it publicly.   The following is the account which Matthew Paris, a writer who lived about those times, has given of the transaction.   " But as the slaughterers of this glorious Martyr had taken an opportunity to slay him from a few words the King had uttered rather imprudently, the King asked absolution from the Bishops who were present at the ceremony, and subjecting his bare skin to the discipline of rods, received four or five stripes from every one of the religious persons, a multitude of whom had assembled.

Another instance of Sovereigns who have been publicly flagellated, may also be reckoned that of Raymond, Count of Toulouse, whose Sovereignty extended over a very considerable part of the South of France.   Having given protection in his dominions to the sect called the Albigenses, Innocent III., the most haughty pope that ever filled the Papal Chair, published a

Croisade against him ; his dominions were in consequence seized, nor could he succeed in having them restored to him before he had submitted to receive discipline from the hands of the Legate of the Pope, who stripped him naked to the waist, at the door of the church, and drove him up to the altar in that situation, all the while beating him with rods.

The last instance of a Sovereign who received a correction from the Church, was that of Henry IV. of France, when he was absolved of his excommunication and heresy ; and the discipline undergone by that Prince supplies the solution for an interesting question, that may be added to those above discussed, viz., Which is the most comfortable manner of receiving a flagellation? —It is by proxy. This was the manner in which the King we speak of suffered the discipline which the Church inflicted upon him. His proxies were Mess. D'Offat and Du Perron, who were afterwards made Cardinals. During the performing of the ceremony of the King's absolution, and while the Choristers were singing the Psalm, *Miserere mei Deus*, the Pope, at every verse, beat with a rod on the shoulders of each of the two proxies ; which shows how essential a part of the ceremony of an absolution flagellations have been thought to be ; and also, how strictly the Church of Rome adheres to such forms as are prescribed by its ritual, or by the *Pontifical*, as it is called. Express mention was moreover made of the above beating, in the written process that was drawn of the transaction. *Dominus Papa verberabat et percutiebat humeros Procuratorum, et cujuslibet ipsorum, virgâ quam in manibus habebat.*

As a further indulgence to the King who was thus disciplined by proxy, and very likely also out of regard for the age in which the ceremony was performed, the two gentlemen who represented him, were suffered to keep their coats on, during the operation ; and the lashes seem, moreover, not to have been laid upon them with any great degree of vigour. However, some persons at the Court of France, either out of envy against the two above gentlemen, on account of the commission with which the King had honoured them, or with a view to divert themselves, had, it seems, circulated a report that on the day of the ceremony, the 17th of September, 1595, they had been made actually to strip in the Church, and undergo a dreadful flagellation. This report M. D'Offat contradicts in one of his letters, the collection of which has been printed; and he says, that the discipline in question was performed to comply with the rules set down in the *Pontifical*, but that "they felt it no more than if it had been a fly that had passed over them, being so well coated as they were."

Very express mention of the above discipline was nevertheless made, as hath been above observed, in the written process drawn on the occasion; though the French Ministers would not suffer it to be joined with the Bull of Absolution, which was sent to the King for his acceptation, and in which no such account was contained. This, another French author observes, did not prevent the Italians from deriving triumph from the event, and saying that the King of France had been disciplined at Rome.

From the above two instances of Henry II. of England and Henry IV. of France (the authenticity of which is beyond any doubt) we find that two crowned heads, Kings of the two most powerful States in Europe, both of the name of Henry, have publicly submitted to the discipline of flagellation, either in their own person or by proxy: the one to preserve his crown, and the other to qualify himself for taking possession of it.

It may be added that an instance of a Sovereign submitting to a flagellation may be seen in our days at every vacancy of the See of Wurtzburgh, a sovereign bishopric in Germany. It is an antient custom in the Chapter of that Church that the person who has been elected to fill the place of the late Bishop, must, before he can obtain his installation, run the gauntlet, naked to the waist, between the Canons, who are formed in two rows and supplied with rods. Some say this custom was established in order to discourage the German Princes from being candidates for the above bishopric; but perhaps also the Canons who established the same had no other design than procuring the pleasure to themselves and successors, when they should afterwards see their equal become their Sovereign, of remembering that they had cudgelled him.

Other facts, besides that of Henry II., show that the power of the clergy was carried as far, at least, in England as in any other country. Bishop Goodwin relates that in the reign of Edward I., Sir Osborn Gifford, of Wiltshire, having assisted in the escape of two nuns from the convent of Wilton, John Peck ham, who was then Archbishop of Canterbury, made him submit, before he absolved him of his excommunication, to be publicly whipped, on three successive Sundays, in the Parish Church of Wilton, and also in the market and church of Shaftesbury.

Chap. VIII.—*A remarkable instance of flagellation performed in honour of the Virgin Mary,*

SO well established was the opinion that saints, and especially the Virgin Mary, were to be appeased by flagellations, and such was in general the fondness of people during a certain period of time for that pious mode of correction, that a Franciscan monk, who wore a hood and was girt with a cord, did not scruple, under the Pontificate of Sixtus IV., to expose to the open day in the public market-place, the bare rump of a Professor of Divinity, and lashed him with his hand in sight of a crowd of astonished spectators, because he had preached against the immaculate conception of the blessed Virgin. The fact is related in a sermon written by Bernardinus de Buftis, which, together with his whole work in honour of the Virgin (Opus Mariale), he dedicated to Pope Alexander VI., and seems therefore to be a fact well enough authenticated. The following is the manner in which Bernardinus gives the account.

"He laid hold of him and threw him upon his knees, for he was very strong. Having then taken up his gown,—because this minister had spoken against the holy tabernacle of God—he began to lash him with the palm of his hand because he had attempted to slander the blessed Virgin by quoting, perhaps, Aristotle in the book of Priors, this preacher confuted him by reading in the book of his posteriors, which greatly diverted the bystanders. Then a certain female devotee exclaimed, saying, "Mr. Preacher, give him four more slaps for my sake," another presently after said, "Give him also four more for me," and so did a number of others, so that if he had attempted to grant all their requests, he would have had nothing else to do for the whole day."

Nay, so proper did Bernardinus de Buftis think the above correction to have been, so well calculated did he judge it to appease the holy Virgin's wrath, that he did not scruple to declare in the sequel of his Sermon, that the monk who had inflicted it had possibly been actuated by an inspiration from the Virgin herself.   "Perhaps," says he, "was it the Virgin herself who induced him so to do, moreover granting him an exemption from the censures incurred, according to the laws of the Church, by those who strike an ecclesiastic, and relaxing the vigour of these laws in his favour."

Another Story of a Female Saint appeased by a Flagellation.

Not only the Virgin Mary but other female saints, inhabitants of Paradise, have also been thought to be extremely well disposed to be appeased when they had received offence by flagellatory corrections.   The following story is to be found in the book entitled, "Itinerarium Cambriæ," wrote by Sylvester Geraldus, a native of the country of Wales, who wrote about the year 1188.

"In the northern borders of England and on the other side of the river Humber, in the parish of Hooëden, lived the rector of that church with his concubine.   This concubine one day sat rather imprudently on the tomb of St. Osanna, sister to King Osred, which was made of wood and raised above the ground in the shape of a seat.   When she attempted to rise from the place she stuck to the wood in such a manner that she never could be parted from it, till, in the presence of the people who ran to see her, she had suffered her clothes to be torn from her, and had received a severe discipline on her naked body, and that to a great effusion of blood, and with many tears and devout supplications on her part; which done, and after she had engaged to submit to further penitence, she was divinely released."

CHAP. IX.—*Formation of the Public Processions of Flagellants. Different success they meet with in different countries.*

THE example which so many illustrious personages had given of voluntarily submitting to flagellation, and the pains which monks had been at to promote that method of mortification by their example likewise, as well as by the stories they related on that subject, had as we have seen, induced the generality of people to adopt the fondest notions of its efficacy. But about the year 1260 the intoxication became as it were complete. People, no longer satisfied to practice mortification of this kind in private, began to perform them in the sight of the public under pretence of greater humiliation; regular associations and fraternities were formed for that purpose, and numerous bodies of half-naked men began to make their appearance in the public streets, who after performing a few religious ceremonies contrived for the occasion, flagellated themselves with astonishing fanaticism and cruelty.

The first institution of public associations and solemnities of this kind must needs have filled with surprise all moderate persons in those days; and in fact we see that historians of different countries who lived in the times when these ceremonies were first introduced, have taken much notice of them, and recorded them at length in their histories or chronicles. I will lay a few extracts of these different books before the reader, it being the best manner, I think, of acquainting him with the origin of these singular flagellating solemnities and processions which continue in use in several countries.

The first author from whom we have a circumstantial account on that subject is the monk of St. Justina, in Padua, whose

Chronicle Wechelius printed afterwards at Basil. He relates how the public superstitious ceremonies we mention made their first appearance in the country in the neighbourhood of Bologna, which is the spot where, it seems, they took their first origin, and whence they were afterwards communicated to other countries. The following is the above author's own account.

"When all Italy was sullied with crimes of every kind, a certain sudden superstition hitherto unknown to the world, first seized the inhabitants of Perusa, afterwards the Romans, and then almost all the nations of Italy. To such a degree were they affected with the fear of God, that noble as well as ignoble persons, young and old, even children five years of age, would go naked about the streets without any sense of shame, walking in public, two and two, in the manner of a solemn procession. Every one of them held in his hand a scourge made of leather thongs, and with tears and groans they lashed themselves on their backs till the blood ran ; all the while weeping and giving tokens of the same bitter affliction as if they had really been spectators of the passion of our Saviour, imploring the forgiveness of God and his Mother, and praying that He who had been appeased by the repentance of so many sinners, would not disdain theirs.

" And not only in the day time but likewise during the nights, hundreds, thousands and tens of thousands of these penitents ran, notwithstanding the rigour of the winter, about the streets and in churches with lighted wax-candles in their hands, and preceded by priests who carried crosses and banners along with them, and with humility prostrated themselves before the altars. The same scenes were to be seen in small towns and villages, so that the mountains and the fields seemed to resound alike the voice of men who were crying to God.

"All musical instruments and love songs then ceased to be heard. The only music that prevailed, both in town and country, was that of the lugubrious voice of the penitent, whose mournful accents might have moved hearts of flint, and even the eyes of the obdurate sinner could not refrain from tears.

"Nor were women exempt from the general spirit of devotion we mention, for not only those among the common people, but also matrons and young maidens of noble families would perform the same mortifications with modesty in their own rooms. Then those who were at enmity with one another became again friends. Usurers and robbers hastened to restore their ill-gotten riches to their right owners. Others, who were contaminated with different crimes, confessed them with humility, and renounced their vanities. Gaols were opened, prisoners were delivered, and banished persons permitted to return to their native habitations. So many and so great works of sanctity and Christian charity, in short, were then performed by both men and women, that it seemed as if an universal apprehension had seized mankind, that the divine power was preparing either to consume them by fire or destroy them by shaking the earth, or some other of those means which divine Justice knows how to employ for avenging crimes.

"Such a sudden repentance which had diffused itself all over Italy and even reached other countries, not only the unlearned, but wise persons also admired. They wondered whence such a vehement fervour of piety could have proceeded; especially since such public penances and ceremonies had been unheard of in former times, had not been approved by the sovereign Pontiff, who was then residing at Anagni, nor recommended by any preacher or person of eminence, but had taken their origin among simple persons, whose example both learned and unlearned had alike followed."

The ceremonies we mention were soon imitated, as the same author remarks, by the other nations of Italy; though they at first met with opposition in several places from divers Princes or Governments in that country. Pope Alexander the Fourth, for instance, who had fixed his See at Anagni, refused at first, as hath been above said, to give his sanction to them; and Clement VI., who had been Archbishop of Sens, in France, in subsequent times condemned those public flagellations by a Bull for that purpose (A. D. 1349). Manfredus, likewise, who was Master of Sicily and Apulia, and Palavicinus, Marquis of Cremona, Brescia and Milan, prohibited the same processions in the countries under their dominion; though, on the other hand, many Princes as well as Popes countenanced them, either in the same times or afterwards.

This spirit of public penance and devotion was in time communicated to other countries; it even reached so far as Greece, as we are informed by Nicephorus Gregoras, who wrote In the year 1361. Attempts were likewise made to introduce ceremonies of the same kind into Poland, as Baronius says in his Annals, but they were at first prohibited; nor did they meet at the same period with more encouragement in Bohemia, as Debravius relates in his History of that country.

In Germany, however, the sect or fraternity of the flagellants, proved more successful. We find a very full account of the first flagellating processions that were made in that country in the year 1349 (a time during which the plague was raging there), in the Chronicle of Albert of Strasbourg, who lived during that period.

"As the plague," says the above author, "was beginning to make its appearance, people then began in Germany to flagellate themselves in public processions. Two hundred came at one time from the country of Schwaben to Spira, having a principal leader at their head, besides two subordinate ones, to whose commands they paid implicit obedience. When they had passed the Rhine at one o'clock in the afternoon, crowds of people ran to see them. They then drew a circular line on the ground, within which they placed themselves. There they stripped off their clothes and only kept upon themselves a kind of short shirt, which served them instead of breeches, and reached from the waist down to their heels; this done, they placed themselves on the above circular line, and began to walk one after another round it, with their arms stretched in the shape of a cross, thus forming among themselves a kind of procession. Having continued this procession a little while, they prostrated themselves on the ground, and afterwards rose one after another in a regular manner, every one of them as he got up, giving a stroke with his scourge to the next, who in his turn likewise rose and served the following one in the same manner. They then began disciplining themselves with their scourges, which were armed with knots and four iron points, all the while singing the usual psalm of the invocation of our Lord, and other psalms; three of them were placed in the middle of the ring, who, with a sonorous voice, regulated the chant of the others, and disciplined themselves in the same manner. This having continued for some time, they ceased their discipline; and then, at a certain signal that was given them, prostrated themselves on their knees, with their arms stretched, and threw themselves flat on the ground, groaning and sobbing. They then rose and heard an admonition from their leader, who exhorted them to implore the mercy of God on the people, on both their benefactors and enemies, and on the souls in Purgatory; then they placed themselves again upon their keees with their hands lifted towards heaven, performed the ceremonies as before, and disciplined themselves anew as they walked round. This done, they put on their clothes again, and those who had been left to take care of the clothes and the luggage came forward and went through the same ceremonies as the former had done. They had among them priests, and noble as well as ignoble persons, and men conversant with letters.

"When the disciplines were concluded one of the brotherhood rose, and with a loud voice read a letter, which he pretended had been brought by an angel to St. Peter's Church, in Jerusalem; the angel declared in it that Jesus Christ was offended at the wickedness of the age, several instances of which were mentioned, such as the violation of the Lord's day, blasphemy, usury, adultery, and neglect with respect to fasting on Fridays. To this the man who read the letter added, that Jesus Christ's forgiveness having been implored by the Holy Virgin and the Angels, he had made answer that in order to obtain mercy, sinners ought to live exiled from their country for thirty-four days, disciplining themselves during that time.

"The inhabitants of the town of Spira were moved with so much compassion for these penitents, that they invited every one of them to their houses; they however refused to receive alms severally, and only accepted what was given to their Society in general, in order to buy twisted wax-candles and banners. These banners were of silk, painted of a purple colour; they carried them in their procession, which they performed twice every day. They never spoke to women, and refused to sleep upon feather beds. They wore crosses upon their coats and hats, behind and before, and had their scourges hanging at their waist.

"About an hundred men in the town of Spira enlisted in their Society, and about a thousand at Strasburg, who promised obedience to the Superiors for the time above mentioned. They admitted nobody but who engaged to observe all the above rules during that time, who could spend at least fourpence a day, lest he should be obliged to beg, and who declared that he had confessed his sins, forgiven his enemies, and obtained the consent of his wife. They divided at Strasburg, one part went up and another part down the country, their Superiors having likewise divided. The latter directed the new brothers from Strasburg not to discipline themselves too harshly in the beginning; and multitudes of people flocked from the country up and down the Rhine, as well as the inland country, in order to see them. After they had left Spira, about two hundred boys twelve years old, entered into an association together, and disciplined themselves in public."

Flagellating processions and solemnities of the same kind were likewise introduced into France, where they met at first with but indifferent success, and even several divines opposed them. The most remarkable among them was John Gerson, a celebrated theologian and Chancellor of the University of Paris, who purposely wrote a treatise against the ceremonies in question, in which he particularly condemned the cruelty and great effusion of blood with which these disciplines were performed. " It is equally unlawful," Gerson asserted, " for a man to draw so much blood from his own body, unless it be for medical reasons, as it would be for him to castrate or otherwise mutilate himself. Else it might upon the same principle be advanced, that a man may brand himself with red-hot irons ; a thing which nobody hath, as yet, either pretended to say or granted, unless it be false Christians and idolaters, such as are to be found in India, who think it a matter of duty for one to be baptized through fire."

Under King Henry the Third, however, the processions of disciplinants found much favour in France ; and the King we mention, a weak and bigoted Prince, not only encouraged these ceremonies by his words, but even went so far as to enlist himself in a Fraternity of Flagellants. The example thus given by the King, procured a great number of associates to the brotherhood ; and several Fraternities were formed at Court, which were distinguished by different colours, and composed of a number of men of the first families in the kingdom. These processions thus formed of the King and his noble train of disciplinants, all equipped like flagellants, frequently made their appearance in the public streets of Paris going from one church to another; and in one of those naked processions the Cardinal of Lorraine, who had joined in it, caught such a cold, it being about Christmas time, that he died a few days afterwards. The following is the account to be found on that subject in President J. A. Thou's "History of his Own Times."

"While the civil war was thus carrying on, scenes of quite a different kind were to be seen at Court, where the King who was naturally of a religious temper, and fond of ceremonies unknown to antiquity, and who had formerly had an opportunity to indulge this fancy in a country subjected to the Pope's dominion, would frequently join in the processions which masked men used to perform on the days before Christmas.

"For more than an hundred years past a fondness for introducing new modes of worship into the established religion had prevailed; and a sect of men had risen, who, thinking it meritorious to manifest the compunction they felt for their offences by outward signs, would put on a sack-cloth in the same manner as it was ordered by the ancient law; and from a strained interpretation they gave of the passage in the Psalmist, *ad flagella paratus sum*, flagellated themselves in public, whence they were called by the name of Flagellants. John Gerson, the Chancellor of the University of Paris and the purest theologian of that age, wrote a book against them. Yet the holy Pontiffs, considering then that sect with more indulgence than the former ones had done, showed much countenance to it; so that multitudes of men all over Italy in these days enlist in it, as in a kind of a religious militia, thinking to obtain by that means forgiveness of their sins.

Distinguished by different colours, blue, white, and black, in the same manner as the Green and Blue Factions, though proposing to themselves different objects, were formerly in Rome they likewise engrossed the attention of the public, and in several places gave rise to the warmest contentions.

"The introduction which was made of these ceremonies into France, where they had till then been almost unknown, forwarded the designs of certain ambitious persons; the contempt they brought on the person of the King having weakened much the regal authority. While the King mixed thus with processions of flagellants, and the most distinguished among his courtiers followed his example, Charles, Cardinal of Lorraine, who was one of the party, was by the coldness of .the evening thrown into a violent fever, attended with a most intense pain in his head; and a delirium as well as continual watchfulness having followed, he expired two days before Christmas."

The historian we have just quoted says in another place, that the King was principally induced to perform the above superstitious processions by the solicitations of his confessor, Father Edmund Auger, who wrote a book on that subject, and of John Castelli, the Apostolic Nuncio in France; and that the weak compliance shown to him on that occasion by the Chancellor Birague, and the Keeper of the Seals, Chiverny, encouraged him much to pursue his plan in that respect, notwithstanding the strong advices to the contrary that were given him by Christopher de Thou, President of the Parliament, and Pierre Brulart, President of the Chambre des Enquêtes.

As there was in those times a powerful party in France that opposed the Court, and even was frequently at open war with it, there was no want of men in Paris who found fault with the disciplining processions of the King. When they first made their appearance, some, as the above historian relates, laughed at them, while others exclaimed that they were an insult both to God and man.   Even preachers joined in the party and pointed their sarcasms from the pulpit against those ceremonies.

The most petulant among these popular preachers was one Maurice Poncer, of the abbey of Melun, who, using expressions borrowed from a psalm, compared the King and his brother disciplinants, to men who would cover themselves with a wet sackcloth to keep off the rain; he was at last banished off to his monastery.   The example which the Court and the Metropolis had set, was followed in a number of country towns, were fraternities of flagellants were instituted; and among them particular mention is made of the brotherhood of the Blue Penitents, in the city of Bourges, on account of the sentence passed in the year 1601 by the Parliament of Paris, in consequence of a motion of Nicholas Servin, the King's Advocate General, which expressly abolished it.

ANECDOTES.

FULK, THE TRAITOR.

THE following is an account of the penance performed by Fulk, surnamed Greisegonnelle, about the year 1000. This Fulk, who was a very powerful man in France, being the son of the great Seneschal of the kingdom, had been a most bad and violent man in those times of feudal anarchy, when force was almost the only law that existed, and when the nobles and lords were rather heads of robbers than persons invested with any precise dignity. Among the crimes the above Fulk had committed, he had killed with his own hand Conan, Duke of Brittany. He had performed three pilgrimages to the Holy Land, and on the last, meaning to render his penance complete, he caused himself to be drawn naked upon a hurdle with a halter round his neck, through the streets of Jerusalem. Men who had been directed so to do, lashed him by turns with scourges; and a person appointed for that purpose cried at certain intervals, "Lord! have mercy on the traitor and forswearer, Fulk." He lived very devoutly, afterwards, and founded several monasteries. An account of this Fulk and his penance, is to be found in Moreri's Dictionary.

ANABAPTISTS.

About the year 1300, a sect of the same kind called the Turlupins (which word rather seems to have been a nickname than a serious appellation of that sect) made their appearance in France, again declaring themselves, as well by their example as by their words, for freedom from accoutrements.   To these the Picards, a century afterwards, succeeded in Germany, who carrying their opinion on the sanctity of nakedness and their abhorrence of such unhallowed thing as clothing, farther than the Adamites had done, made at all times their appearance in a perfect state of nature.   A certain party of Anabaptists adopting the doctrine of these Picards, tried, on the thirteenth day of February in the year 1535, to make an excursion in the streets of Amsterdam, in the hallowed state we mention; but the Magistracy, not taking the joke so well as they ought to have done, used these adventurers in rather a severe manner.

———

The Boston Magistrates and the Captain.

The following story which is given in the writer's own words gives a curious insight into the puritanical manners that prevailed in the New England Provinces.   About forty years ago many of the Chief Saints at Boston met with a sad mortification, yea, a mortification in the flesh.

"Captain St. Loe, Commander of the ship of war, then in Boston Harbour, being ashore on a Sunday, was apprehended by the Constables for walking on the Lord's Day.   On Monday he was carried before a Justice of the Peace, he was fined, refused to pay it; and for his contumacy and contempt of authority, was sentenced to sit in the stocks one hour during the time of change.   This sentence was put in execution without the least mitigation.

"While the Captain sat in durance, grave Magistrates admonished him to respect in future the wholesome laws of the Province; and Reverend Divines exhorted him ever after to reverence and keep holy the Sabbath-day.   At length the hour expired; and the Captain's legs were set at liberty.

"As soon as he was freed, he, with great seeming earnestness, thanked the Magistrates for their correction, and the Clergy for their spiritual advice and consolation; declaring that he was ashamed of his past life; that he was resolved to put off the old Man of Sin, and to put on the new Man of Righteousness; that he should ever pray for them as instruments in the hands of God, of saving his sinful soul.

"This sudden conversion rejoiced the Saints. After clasping their hands, and casting up their eyes to heaven, they embraced their new Convert, and returned thanks for being made the humble means of snatching a soul from perdition. Proud of their success, they fell to exhorting him afresh; and the most zealous invited him to dinner, that they might have full time to complete their work.

"The Captain sucked in the milk of exhortation, as a new-born babe does the milk of the breast. He was as ready to listen as they were to exhort. Never was a Convert more assiduous, while his station in Boston Harbour lasted: he attended every Sabbath-day their most sanctified meeting house; never missed a weekly lecture; at every private Conventicle, he was most fervent and loudest in prayer. He flattered, and made presents to the wives and daughters of the godly. In short, all the time he could spare from the duties of his station, was spent in entertaining them on board his ship, or in visiting and praying at their houses.

"The Saints were delighted with him beyond measure. They compared their wooden stocks to the voice of Heaven, and their sea-convert to St. Paul; who, from their enemy, was become their doctor.

"Amidst their mutual happiness, the mournful time of parting arrived. The Captain received his recall. On this he went round among the godly, and wept and prayed, assuring them he would return, and end his days among his friends in the Lord.

"Till the day of his departure, the time was spent in regrets, processions, entertainments, and prayer. On that day, about a dozen of the principal Magistrates, including the Select-men, accompanied the Captain to Nantasket Road, where the ship lay, with everything ready for sailing.

"An elegant dinner was provided for them on board; after which many bowls and bottles were drained. As the blood of the Saints waxed warm, the crust of their hypocrisy melted away; their moral see-saws and Scripture texts gave place to double-entendres and wanton songs; the Captain encouraged their gaiety, and the whole ship resounded with the roar of their merriment.

"Just at that time into the cabin burst a body of sailors, who, to the inexpressible horror and amazement of the Saints, pinioned them fast. Heedless of cries and entreaties they dragged them upon deck, where they were tied up, stripped to the buff, and their breeches let down; and the boatswain with his assistants, armed with dreadful cat-o'-nine-tails provided for the occasion, administered unto them the law of Moses in the most energetic manner. Vain were all their prayers, roarings, stampings, and curses; the Captain in the meantime assuring them that it was consonant to their own doctrine and to Scripture, that the mortification of the flesh tended towards the saving of the soul, and therefore it would be criminal in him to abate them a single lash.

"When they had suffered the whole of their discipline, which had flayed them from the nape of the neck to the hams, the Captain took a polite leave, earnestly begging them to remember him in their prayers. They were then let down into the boat that was waiting for them, the crew saluted them with three cheers, and Captain St. Loe made sail."

Lady Liancourt.

An account contained in the collection of " Celebrated Causes " decided in the French Courts of Law, is given of a case in the reign of Louis the Fourteenth, which made a very great noise. The case referred to is the flagellation that was served by the Marchioness de Tresnel on the Dame or Lady of Liancourt, a fact which by all means deserves a place in this volume, as being in itself an extremely illustrious instance of flagellation. Indeed, one advantage the author is proud of, which is, that he has inserted nothing vulgar in this book, nothing but what is worthy of taste and sentiment.

The story is as follows. The Lady of Liancourt was originally born of parents in middling circumstances. Having had the good luck to marry a rich merchant, she had address enough to prevail upon him to bequeath to her at his death—which happened a few years after their marriage—the bulk of his fortune; and being now a rich handsome widow, she married the Sieur or Lord of Liancourt, a man of birth, whose fortune was somewhat impaired by his former expensive way of living. The Lady of Liancourt used to reside during the summer at the castle or estate of her husband, near the town of Chaumont, and in the same neighbourhood was situated the estate of the Marquis of Tresnel. The manner of living of the Lady of Liancourt, together with the reputation of her wit and beauty, excited the jealousy of the Marchioness of Tresnel, who, on account of her birth, considered herself as being greatly superior to the other; and a strong competition soon took place between the two ladies, which became manifested in several places in a remarkable manner, especially at church, where the Marchioness once went so far as violently to push the other lady from her seat. The Lady of Liancourt, on the other hand, was said to have written a copy of verses against the

Marchioness; and, in short, matters were carried to such lengths between them, that the Marchioness resolved to damp at once the pretentions of her rival, and for that purpose applied to that effectual mode of correction which, as hath been seen in the course of this book, so many great and celebrated personages have undergone, namely, a flagellation. Having well laid her scheme in that respect, and resolved that her rival should undergo the correction not by proxy, like King Henry the Fourth, but in her own person,—the Marchioness, one day she knew the Lady of Liancourt was to visit at a castle a few miles distant from her own, got into her coach and six, accompanied by four men behind and three armed servants on horseback; and care had been previously taken to lay in a stock of good disciplines, which were placed in the coach-box. Having arrived too late at the place on the highway at which she proposed to meet her antagonist, the Marchioness alighted at the house of the Curate of the parish in order to wait for her return, and stayed there under some pretence, several hours, till at last a servant who had been on the watch, came in haste and brought tidings that the Lady Liancourt's coach was in sight. The Marchioness thereupon got into her coach with the utmost speed, and arrived just in time to throw herself across the way and stop the other lady; when the servants, who had been properly directed beforehand, without loss of time took the latter out of the coach, immediately proceeding to execute the orders they had received; and from the complaint afterwards preferred by the suffering lady, it really seems that they endeavoured to discharge their duty in such a manner as might convince their mistress of their zeal in serving her.

The affair soon made a great noise, and the King, who heard it, immediately sent express orders to the husbands of the ladies to take no share in the quarrel. The Lady of Liancourt applied to the ordinary course of law and brought a criminal action against the Marchioness before the Parliament of Paris; the consequence of which was that the latter was condemned to ask her pardon in the open Court upon her knees, and to pay her about two hundred pounds damages, besides being banished from the whole extent of the jurisdiction of the Parliament. The servants, who are generally very severely dealt with in France when they suffer themselves to become the instruments of the violence of their masters, were sent to the Gallies.

THE BITER BIT.

A lady of rank who had a perfect passion for flagellating both her slaves and her children, used to flog some one every day of her life, always with her own hand. She had a kind of block erected where she had them stretched, and nothing pleased her more than to see them writhing under the lash. One day she had carried her passion to such a degree as to have the whole household flogged. This was the culmination of her flogging glories, for her severity raised a revolt, and the slaves combining seized upon the mistress and tying her to the block, each one of them administered five blows upon her person with any of the scourges they pleased.

THE CHINESE.

A remarkable instance of this power of use, to enable us to bear hardships, and even blows, occurs among the Chinese. It appears, from the accounts of travellers, that there are men in China who make it their trade, being properly feed for it, to receive the bastinadoes in the room of those who are sentenced to it by the Mandarine; in the same manner as there are men about the Courts of Law in this Country, ready to bail upon any occasion. As the bastinadoe is inflicted on the spot, while the Mandarine is dispatching other business, the thing is to bribe the Officer who is to superintend the operation: the real Culprit then slips out of the way; the man who is to do duty for him comes forth, suffers himself to be tied down to the ground, and receives the bastinadoe; which is laid on in such earnest, that a fresh man, or executioner, is employed after every ten or twenty strokes.

THE ARABIAN TALES.

In one of the Arabian Tales, called "The one thousand and one Nights:" an original book, and which contains true pictures of the manners of that nation, is a story which is well worth reminding the reader of, that of a certain Cobler, whose name, if I mistake not, was Shak-Abak. This Cobler having fallen in love with a beautiful lady belonging to some wealthy man, or man of power, of whom he had had a glance through the window of her house, would afterwards keep for whole hours every day, staring at the window. The lady, who proposed to make game of him, one day sent one of her female slaves to introduce him to her, and then gave him to understand, that if he could overtake her, by running after her through the apartments of her house, he would have the pleasure of her company; he was besides told, that in order to run more nimbly, he must strip to the shirt. To all this Shak-Abak agreed: and after a number of turns up and down the house, he was at last enticed into a long, dark, and narrow passage, at the farthest extremity of which an open door was to be perceived; he made to it as fast as he could, and when he had reached it, rushed headlong through it; when, to his no small astonishment, the door instantly shut upon him, and he found himself in the middle of a public street of Bagdat, which was chiefly inhabited by shoemakers. A number of these latter, struck at the sudden and strange appearance of the unfortunate Shak-Abak, who, besides stripping to his shirt, had suffered his eye-brows to be shaved, laid hold of him, and, as the Arabian Author relates, soundly lashed him with their straps.

———

Various stories were given out by the monks of the chastisement received by persons who had persecuted them. This misfortune happened to a certain servant of the Emperor Nicephorus, who, not satisfied with exacting unjust tributes from the common people with great rigour, offered afterwards to use the monasteries in the same manner. " The Emperor," says the author from whom this fact is extracted, "sent one of the grooms of his bedchamber to receive the usual tribute. As he was a man exceedingly eager after money and unlawful gain, he committed great oppressions both on the common citizens and the inhabitants of the monastery of St. Nicon ; for the government of cities and the care of levying duties are usually entrusted, not to the just and mild, but to hard-harded and inhuman persons. The monks, who were possessed of no money, endeavoured to soothe the above unmerciful man by their discourses ; but he, thirsty after gold, was as deaf to their prayers as the asp to conjurations, and made no more account of their remonstrances, than, to use the words of Scripture, of " the crackling of thorns under a pot." On the contrary, his wrath and insolence increased farther, he caused several of them to be thrown into a jail, and prepared to plunder the monastery. The remaining monks then applied to their Saint for assistance, who presently made them experience the happy effects of it; for during the following night he appeared to the groom with a threatening indignant aspect, and lashed him severely; then speaking to him, told him, for his words ought to be recorded: 'Thou hast thrown the heads of the monastery into chains, if thou dost not release them instantly, thy death shall be the consequence.'"

It was politely adopted in Denmark, and even in the Court of that country, towards the latter end of the last century, as we are informed by Lord Molesworth, in his "Account of Denmark." It was the custom, his Lordship says, at the end of every hunting-match at Court, that, in order to conclude the entertainment with as much festivity as it had begun, a proclamation was made,—if any could inform against any person who had infringed the known laws of hunting, let him stand forth and accuse. As soon as the contravention was ascertained, the culprit was made to kneel down between the horns of the stag that had been hunted; two of the gentlemen removed the skirts of his coat; when the King, taking a small long wand in his hand, laid a certain number of blows, which was proportioned to the greatness of the offence, on the culprit; whilst, in the meantime (the noble author adds) the huntsmen with their brass horns, and the dogs with their loud openings, proclaimed the King's justice and the criminal's punishment.

In Spain, when gentlemen proposed to discipline themselves in honour of their mistresses, and were of considerable rank, the ceremony was performed with great state and magnificence. Madame D'Aunoy relates that the day the Duke of Vejar disciplined himself, an hundred white wax candles were carried before the procession: the Duke was preceded by sixty of his friends (vassals perhaps, or dependents) and followed by an hundred, all attended by their own pages and footmen; and besides them there were no doubt abundance of priests and crucifixes.

As these Spanish gallants have no less honour than devotion, battles frequently take place between them, for the assertion of their just prerogatives; and this, for instance, seldom fails to be the case when two processions happen to meet in the same street: each party think they are intitled to the most honourable side of the way; and a scuffle is the consequence. This happened at the time of the procession of the above-mentioned Duke of Vejar: another procession, conducted by the Marquis of Villa-hermosa, entered the same street, at the other end of it: the light-armed troops, otherwise the servants with their lighted long wax candles, began the engagement, bedaubing the clothes, and singeing the whiskers and hair of each other; then the body of infantry, that is to say the gentlemen with their swords, made their appearance, and continued the battle; and at last the two noble champions themselves met, and began a fight with their disciplines. Another instance of penitents using their disciplines as weapons, is to be found in Don Quixote (where two noble champions began a smart engagement with each other); their self-flagellations were for a while changed, with great rapidity, into mutual ones, and their weapons being demolished, they were about to begin a closer kind of fight, when their friends interfered, and parted them: the high, sharp, and stiff cap of one of the two combatants, which had fallen in the dirt, was taken up, properly cleansed, and again placed upon his head; and the two processions went each their own course, dividing as chance determined it. The whole ceremony was afterwards concluded with splendid entertainments which each of the noble discipliants gave in their houses, to the persons who had formed their respective processions, during which abundance of fine compliments were paid them on their piety, their gallantry, and their elegance in giving themselves discipline.

———

A certain friar, in a convent of the Benedictine Order, found means to procure, besides plenty of good wine, a certain number of dishes extremely nice and well seasoned, several of which were expressly forbidden by the institutes of the Order; and he invited a select party of brothers to partake of his fare. As they could not, with any degree of safety, carry on the entertainment in the cell of any of them, they thought of repairing to one of the cellars of the house, where they hid themselves in one of those wide and shallow tuns (about eight or nine feet in diameter, and three or four deep) which serve in the making of wines. The Abbot, in the meanwhile, missing so many of the monks from the convent, went in search of them through all the different apartments: being unable to find them, he at last went down into the cellars, and soon perceived whereabout they lay: he stepped up to the place, and, on a sudden, made his appearance over the edge of the tun. The monks were prodigiously alarmed at this unexpected appearance of the Abbot; and there was none among them but who would have gladly compromised the affair, by giving up his remaining share of the entertainment, and submitting to instant dismission. But the Abbot, contrary to all hope, put on a mild and cheerful look; he kindly expostulated with the monks on their having made a secret of the affair to him; expressed to them the great pleasure it would have been for him to be one of their party; and added, that he should still be very glad to be admitted to partake of the entertainment. The monks answered, by all means: the Abbot thereupon leaped into the tun ; sat down among them ; partook of their excellent wine and well-seasoned dishes with the greatest freedom ; and, in short, spent an hour or two with them in the tun, in the most agreeable and convivial manner.

At last the Abbot thought proper to withdraw, and as soon as he had taken his leave, some of the monks began to admire his extraordinary condescension, while the others were not without fears that it foreboded some misfortune. Indeed, the latter were in the right; for the reader must not think that the Abbot had acted in the manner above described, out of any sudden temptation he had felt at the sight of the jollity of the friars, or of the dainties that composed the entertainment : by no means ; his design had only been, by thus making himself guilty along with them, to be the better able to show them afterwards the way to repentance, and thereby derive good from evil. In fact, the next day, a chapter having been summoned, the Abbot desired the Prior to fill his place, while himself took his seat among the rest of the monks. Soon after the chapter was met, he stepped forward into the middle of the assembly, accused himself of the sin he had committed the day before, and requested that discipline might be inflicted upon him. The Prior objected much to a discipline being inflicted on the Abbot; but the latter having insisted, his request was complied with. The other monks were at first greatly astonished, but seeing no possibillity of keeping back on that occasion, they stepped into the middle of the chapter, and likewise confessed their sin ; when the Abbot, by means of a proper person he had selected for the purpose, got a lusty discipline to be inflicted upon every one of his late fellow-banqueters.

The celebrated fathers of St. Lazare, in Paris, whose school was otherwise named the "Seminary of the good Boys" *(des bons enfans)* have no less recommended themselves by the regularity of the disciplines they inflicted, than the Reverend Father Jesuits. They were even superior to the latter, in regard to those recommendatory flagellations mentioned above, which were administered to such persons as were, by some means or other, induced to deliver letters to the fathers for that purpose. Being situated in the metropolis, the seminary carried on a very extensive business in that way. Fathers or mothers who had undutiful sons, tutors who had unruly pupils, uncles who were instructed with the education of ungovernable nephews, masters who had wickedly-inclined apprentices, whom they durst not themselves undertake to correct, applied to the fathers of St. Lazare, and by properly feeing them, had their wishes gratified. Indeed the fathers had found means to secure their doors with such good bolts, they were so well stocked with the necessary implements for giving disciplines, and had such a numerous crew of stout Cuiftres to inflict them, that they never failed to execute any job they had engaged to perform, and without minding either age, courage, or strength, were at all times ready to undertake the most difficult flagellations. So regular was the trade carried on, by the good fathers in that branch of business, that letters of the above kind directed to them, were literally notes of hand payable on sight ; and provided such notes did but come to hand, whoever the bearer might be, the fathers were sure to have them discharged with punctuality.

This kind of business, as it was carried on for a number of years, frequently gave rise to accidents, or mistakes, of rather a ludicrous kind. Young men who had letters to carry to the house of St. Lazare, the contents of which they did not mistrust, would often undesignedly charge other persons to carry the

same for them, either on account of their going to that part
of the town, or for some other reason of a like kind: and the
unfortunate bearer, who suspected no harm, had no sooner
delivered the dangerous letter with which he had suffered himself
to be instructed, than he was collared, and rewarded for his
good-nature by a severe and unexpected flagellation.

Ladies, it is likewise said, who had been forsaken, or otherwise
ungenteelly used by their admirers, when every other means of
revenge failed, would also recur to the ministry of the fathers of
St. Lazare. Either by making interest with other persons, or
using some artfully-contrived scheme, the provoked fair one
endeavoured to have the gentleman who caused her grief,
inveigled into the house of the seminary: at the same time she
took care to have a letter to recommend him, sent there from
some unknown quarter, with proper fees in it; for that was a
point that must not be neglected: and when the gentleman came
afterwards to speak with the fathers, he was no sooner found by
them, either from the nature of the business he said he came
upon, or other marks, to be the person mentioned in the letter
they had before received, than they shewed him into an adjoining
room, where this treacherous and deceitful lover was immediately
seized, mastered, and everything in short was performed that was
requisite to procure ample satisfaction to the fair injured lady.

It is also said (for a number of stories are related on that subject, and the Seminary of St. Lazare was become for a while an
object of terror to all Paris) that schemes of the most abusive
kind were in latter times carried on, through the connivance
which the fathers began to show at the knavery of certain persons; and this indeed seems to be a well-ascertained part of the
story. Abuses of the same kind as those which once prevailed
in mad-houses established in this country, were at last practised

in the seminary. Men possessed of estates which some near relations wanted to enjoy, or whom it was the interest of other persons to keep for a while out of the way, were inveigled into the House of Lazare, where they were detained, and large sums paid monthly for their board.

FINIS.